WISCONSIN
HEROES

Marv Balousek

Waubesa Press
P.O. Box 192
Oregon, WI 53575

© Copyright 1995 by Marvin W. Balousek Jr.
Published by Waubesa Press of Oregon, WI
Editing/proofreading by J. Allen Kirsch
Color separations by Port to Print of Madison, WI
Printed by BookCrafters of Chelsea, MI

Cover illustration from electronically enhanced versions of photos used by permission of Madison Newspapers Inc. newsroom library and State Historical Society of Wisconsin.

First Edition

ISBN 1-878569-28-7

Publisher's Cataloging in Publication
(Prepared by Quality Books Inc.)

Balousek, Marv W., 1948-
    Wisconsin heroes / Marv Balousek
    p. cm.
    Includes bibliographical references and index.
    ISBN: 1-878569-28-7

    1. Wisconsin—Biography.   I. Title.
F586.4.B35 1995   977.5'009'92
                               QBI95-20452

For my heroes: Marvin (Sr.) and Frances Balousek;
Bob Balousek; and Barbara Snell.

Contents

Chapter 30
Woman of the century

Introduction

After writing two books about Wisconsin's worst crimes, I have decided to turn over a new leaf and write instead about the state's heroes.

It was a task I discovered was far more difficult that writing about crimes and criminals. In researching a crime, I often had day after day of trial coverage to draw upon. But a heroic rescue often merits only a brief mention in a daily newspaper, if at all. Although we could bemoan the fact that criminals outweigh heroes in press coverage, we can be comforted that this means we still view criminals as aberrations and crime as unusual.

I use the word *hero* to refer to all, instead of designating women as *heroines*. After all, *Hero* in Greek mythology was a woman, a legendary priestess of Aphrodite loved by Leander.

The greatest difficulty in writing this book, however, was not in the research but in the selection. Wisconsin has a generous supply of heroes, both famous and obscure, including men, women and animals. I have tried to select representative heroes from areas including war, sports, politics and outer space exploration. I also have included 10 chapters on lifesaving heroes who are not very well known. These are men and women who received awards from the Carnegie Hero Fund Commission.

Wisconsin has produced more than its share of astronauts, including two who are profiled here. They are James Lovell of Milwaukee, commander of the ill-fated Apollo 13 mission, and Donald "Deke" Slayton of Sparta, one of the original Mercury 7 astronauts.

Two women are honored through school observance days designated by the Legislature but their stories are not well known. They are Mildred Fish Harnack, the only American executed by Hitler, and Frances Willard, who served as national president of the Women's Christian Temperance Union during the late 19th Century.

The state also has a long list of winners of the Congressional Medal of Honor. Three of them include Richard Bong of Poplar, a pilot who set a World War II killing record that probably never will be surpassed; Gary Wetzel of Oak Creek, a Vietnam War hero who later saved a man from a burning car; and Mitchell Red Cloud of Friendship, a hero of the Korean War. Another war hero profiled in this book is Old Abe, the legendary Civil War eagle.

Selecting political heroes is dangerous and can become marred by partisanship but I believe there is little question that Belle and Robert La Follette or Golda Meir are among Wisconsin's greatest heroes.

The personal stories of Bonnie Blair and Dan Jansen are well known. There is no question that both are two of Wisconsin's sports heroes. But instead of profiling them, I have written about Dianne Holum. Beyond her own championship skating, she also was a championship coach. Among her students were many of the state's Olympic medal winners, including Eric and Beth Heiden.

Elroy "Crazy Legs" Hirsch's tenure as University of Wisconsin athletic director didn't produce many great teams. But Hirsch was a collegiate football star of the early 1940s who later battled back from serious injury to reclaim his professional career.

Police officers and firefighters often are called upon for heroic deeds. Many police officers have died in the line of duty. Two officers, however, who didn't die but unquestionably saved lives were Louis Molnar of Madison and Russell Cera of Racine. Three of Wisconsin's most heroic firefighters were on the scene of a Milwaukee tunnel cave-in early in the century.

Other heroes I have profiled include James Stout, a national pioneer of vocational education; Cordelia Harvey, a governor's wife who persuaded Abraham Lincoln to build veterans' hospitals in the North; Al Ringing, the master showman who founded the Ringling Brothers Circus; and Howard Temin, a Nobel Prize-winning cancer researcher.

I want to thank Walter Rutkowski of the Carnegie Hero Fund Commission who generously supplied information about Wisconsin award winners. Fannie Hicklin of the State Historical Society also gave me a long list of state heroes. My colleague at *The Capital Times* of Madison, Mike Miller, suggested profiles of Mildred Fish Harnack and Frances Willard.

Ron Larson, the newsroom librarian at Madison Newspapers, was very helpful in giving me access to clip files and photographs. I also want to thank my *Wisconsin State Journal* colleague, George Hesselberg, for information he supplied about Louis Molnar.

In the introductions to my two crime books, I suggested that studying crime and criminals can give us insight into prevention. This book, however, profiles people we can strive to emulate. If there is one quality shared by all of the figures in this book, it is self-sacrifice — a willingness to put the lives or well-being of others ahead of themselves.

Marv Balousek
September 1995

Chapter 1

Hero of Apollo 13

James A. Lovell Jr.

When James A. Lovell Jr. rode the streetcar around Milwaukee with Marilyn Gerlach, his high school sweetheart, he often would look up at the stars, pointing out and naming constellations for her. When he was even younger, Lovell once built a homemade model rocket that blew up on the launch pad.

A longtime dream of Lovell's was to walk on the moon. After years as a Navy test pilot and astronaut, he finally got his chance but a near tragedy prevented it.

Lovell was born in Cleveland but his parents moved to their Milwaukee home on North 35th Street when he was nine years old. After graduating from Juneau High School, he married Marilyn Gerlach and went on to have four children: Barbara, James, Susan and Jeffrey.

Lovell spent two years as a mechanical engineering student at the University of Wisconsin. In 1948, he attended the Aviation Safety School at the University of Southern California and received a bachelor's degree in 1952 from the United States Naval Academy.

He worked three years as a test pilot at the Naval Air Test Center at Patuxent River, Maryland. He also served as a flight instructor and safety officer at the Naval Air Station in Oceana, Virginia.

In 1962, Lovell applied for the astronaut program. He underwent nine days of medical and psychological testing plus a series of interviews. In September, he was among nine astronauts selected to begin training for the Apollo missions to the moon. By the time he became an astronaut, Lovell had logged 2,300 of flying time, including over 1,600 hours in jet aircraft.

He was selected as the pilot of the backup crew on the Gemini 4 mission. Then, in December 1965, he flew on the Gemini 7 flight with Frank Borman. The two men orbited the earth for two weeks, setting a world endurance record. But the real accomplishment of the fourteen-day mission was a rendezvous with the Gemini 6 spacecraft manned by Walter Schirra and Thomas Stafford.

Lovell piloted the Gemini 12 mission in November 1966 and watched through the window as his crew mate, Maj. Edwin "Buzz" Aldrin Jr., walked in space.

Among those on hand to watch the historic Apollo 8 launch in December 1968 were Charles Lindbergh and U.S. Sen. Edward Kennedy. More than 250,000 spectators, the largest crowd ever, watched the Saturn 5 rocket lift off the Cape Canaveral launch pad, carrying Lovell, Borman and William Anders. Lindbergh, the first airplane pilot to take a solo flight across the Atlantic Ocean, often watched spacecraft lift-offs during the 1960s.

During their ten lunar orbits on Christmas Eve and Christmas Day, the three astronauts became the first men to see the back side of the moon. The spacecraft lost contact with earth while traveling behind the moon.

Lovell, Borman and Anders also became the first humans to leave earth's gravity and experience that of the moon.

World Book Encyclopedia Science Service

James Lovell Jr. in test pilot gear (1960 photo).

Preparing for re-entry, the crew had plenty of time for joking with ground controllers:

"We're now looking at Texas," Lovell reported at one point.

"Can you see the kids out in the yard waving?" asked controller Jerry Carr.

"Tell (astronaut) Pete Conrad to get his kids off my roof," Lovell quipped.

Ten lunar orbits had brought Lovell closer to his personal goal of walking on the moon. For the Apollo 11 flight, however, he would remain in the wings while astronaut Neil Armstrong became the first man to walk on the moon.

"Contrary to people who wanted to believe that there were giant monsters on the moon, the lunar surface was exactly as we had suspected it would be," said Lovell, who supported the crew from Mission Control. "I was very happy and elated. The goal had been reached."

But Lovell's personal goal was yet to be met. On the Apollo 13 mission, it looked as if he finally would get his chance to set foot on the lunar surface. Lovell, who held the record for the most time in space, said it would be his last mission.

"There are a lot of people standing in line for flights," he said. "I've had more than my share."

Lovell, joined on the flight by civilian astronauts John Swigert and Fred Haise, also said the moon landing mission "embodies everything I've learned." Swigert was a last-minute replacement for Thomas Mattingly, who had been exposed to the German measles and was in danger of coming down with the disease.

A superstitious person might find some significance that the four-day Apollo 13 mission got under way on April 13, 1970. The lift-off was uneventful and the astronauts turned their ship toward their lunar destination.

Three days into the flight, however, when the astronauts were more than 200,000 miles from earth, ground controllers noticed a sharp increase in pressure in a service module. They also noticed that relief valves weren't opening to relieve the pressure.

In the spacecraft, Lovell and his crew members heard a loud bang while the ground controllers monitored a pressure drop. An explosion of oxygen occurred in the service module, not the command module where the astronauts worked and slept. But the explosion portended certain disaster for the mission. The now useless service module contained essential oxygen, water and propellant for the mission. A more crucial loss, however, was that the explosion knocked out the power for the command ship. For all practical purposes, the three unlucky astronauts appeared stranded in space without enough water or oxygen to keep them alive for very long. As a result, the moon landing was scrubbed and the more difficult task would be getting the three astronauts back to earth.

"I'm disappointed that they can't land on the moon and my only concern now is that they can safely return home," said a worried Marilyn Lovell.

At Mission Control, technicians worked feverishly to find a way to bring the men back to earth. Despite deep political divisions over the Vietnam War, the nation joined together in prayer vigils for the three endangered astronauts. President Richard Nixon cancelled entertainment at a state dinner so he could stay informed about Apollo 13 developments. The front page of the April 17, 1970, edition of the *Wisconsin State*

Journal carried only a sketch of the three astronauts and the two-inch headline: Let us all pray for their safe return.

In the spacecraft, an ominous chill began to set in. The temperature in the command module became so cold that the three astronauts huddled together in the lunar module, which still had power.

"Now you know why we call it the refrigerator," Swigert said during one transmission.

If the lunar module could land on the moon, perhaps it could help bring the astronauts back to earth. Firing up the lunar module's engine caused a key course adjustment that headed the spacecraft toward home.

Re-entry, however, would involve more timing and ingenuity than on other flights. It would require perfect timing in separating the service module and jettisoning the lunar module as the frigid command module with the three astronauts hurtled through the atmosphere.

After a harrowing final four days of the mission, Lovell, Swigert and Haise splashed down safely and millions of people breathed a collective sigh of relief.

The three astronauts escaped with their lives even though Lovell had failed to achieve his dream. He kept his vow, however, and retired from the space program.

His popularity as a national hero started Wisconsin Republicans talking about Lovell as a candidate against U.S. Sen. William Proxmire from Wisconsin, who was seeking his third term. Lovell didn't discount future political ambitions but declined to run that time.

A month after the mission ended, the nation's solidarity in praying for the astronauts safe return apparently had melted. Student unrest on the University of Wisconsin-Madison campus caused relocation of a dinner where Lovell was the featured speaker.

In 1975, Lovell, chairman of the president's Council on Physical Fitness and Sports, wrote a syndicated newspaper article urging people to quit smoking, exercise and make healthy dietary changes. "If we don't," he wrote, "I'm convinced that the last human sound on this continent won't be a bang, but a burp."

In 1976, Lovell was named president of Fisk Telephone Systems of Houston and, later that year, he withdrew as a candidate for president of the Milwaukee School of Engineering.

The Apollo 13 mission fueled a growing public skepticism about the space program and, although there were more Apollo missions, the space program clearly had passed its peak in popularity.

"Space, in a way, is a dream," the *Wisconsin State Journal* editorialized during the Apollo 13 mission. "And without dreams and attempts to make them real, where would man be?"

Chapter 2

Literary dissident
Mildred Fish Harnack

In the dankness of her Nazi prison cell, Mildred Fish Harnack scribbled down poetry to keep herself sane. The verses helped her remember her homeland so far away from the alien nation where she had been arrested and jailed.

When lilacs last in the dooryard bloom'd, she wrote, recalling the words of American poet Walt Whitman. *And the great star early droop'd in the western sky at night. I mourn'd, and yet shall mourn with ever-returning spring.*

Meanwhile, Adolph Hitler paged through court records, fascinated by reports on those who had defied his regime by daring to challenge his claim to world power through underground organizations. He had vowed to root them all out. Suddenly, he stopped when he came across Harnack's name. Poring over her dossier, Hitler noticed she was an American. He also noticed that, despite her crimes, she had gotten off with a light sentence of six months of hard labor.

The Führer was outraged. Why should this woman escape the guillotine? Especially when she gave him the perfect opportunity to strike back personally at the hated Americans, who had joined the war a little more than a year earlier.

Hitler summoned Manfred Roeder, the Nazi chief judge who had decreed the original sentence. Although Hitler had ordered Harnack's light sentence originally, he now changed his mind, demanding that Roeder change the sentence to death.

Mildred Fish Harnack wouldn't see another Whitman spring. She was beheaded on Feb. 16, 1943, several weeks after her husband, Arvid, was hanged on Christmas Eve, 1942. At age 40, she became the only American woman executed by the Gestapo.

As her ability to summon up great poetry in her cell would indicate, she was no common criminal. She grew up in Milwaukee, then attended the University of Wisconsin in Madison. After her graduation in 1925, she joined the English faculty.

In 1926, she met Arvid Harnack, a German student whom she eventually married. In 1930, the couple moved to Germany.

But Germany in the 1930s was not an easy place to live for intellectuals like the Harnacks. Hitler's ever-increasing efforts to control public thought and behavior infuriated the couple and others. As the 1940s dawned, Germany was at war and dissenters like Arvid Harnack became involved in underground organizations determined to oust Hitler.

Mildred Harnack joined her husband in the underground movement, typing and distributing leaflets, keeping contact with members and arranging secret meetings. They became active members of the Schulze-Boysen resistance group, better known to the Gestapo by the code name of the Red Orchestra. The Harnacks were Gentiles but risked their lives to save hundred of Jews from execution. After months of clandestine activity, luck finally ran out and they were arrested in September 1942.

In her cell, the poetry helped lift Mildred Harnack's spirits as she awaited Hitler's verdict. Besides Whitman's *When Lilacs Last in the Dooryard Bloom'd,* she also left behind scribbled verses from Shelley's *Adonais.*

Shortly after her death, a personal friend recognized Mildred Harnack's headless torso and quickly removed it. In a final act of defiance, her body was cremated and the ashes were taken to the home of her sister-in-law in Berlin.

On Sept. 22, 1946, exactly four years after the Harnacks were arrested, 10,000 Berliners gathered at the Luftgarten to pay tribute to the dissident men and women who died on Hitler's guillotine. Imprinted on a long black banner were the words: "To Honor the Dead — and to Remind the Living."

A school in East Berlin was named after Mildred Harnack and a street was named after her husband. Along with Frances Willard, she is one of two women that Wisconsin students are required by statute to study.

After Germany reunited in 1991, changes in street

names were proposed to wipe out any memory of the socialist regime. Samson Knoll, a California professor, wrote President George Bush in an effort to persuade German officials to keep as many names as possible in honor of the resistance fighters.

In 1994, Mildred Fish Harnack's story was featured in a lecture series on human rights at the University of Wisconsin, where she had taught English nearly seventy years earlier. A lecture titled *Resister, Martyr, Scholar, Spy: Mildred Fish Harnack Through History* was delivered by Shareen Blair Brysac, a New York writer and producer-director of documentary films.

I saw battle-corpses, myriads of them,
And the white skeletons of young men, I saw them.
I saw the debris and debris of all slain soldiers of the war.
But I saw they were not as was thought,
They themselves were fully at rest, they suffer'd not.
The living remain'd and suffer'd, the mother suffer'd,
And the wife and the child and the musing comrade suffer'd,
And the armies that remain'd suffer'd.

— Walt Whitman
When Lilacs Last in the Dooryard Bloom'd

Chapter 3

Rescue of little Emma

Edward McGrath

Shortly before noon on the balmy day of Aug. 26, 1907, little Emma Humich started out from her home at 841 Clinton Ave. in Milwaukee on a routine trip to the candy store. The five-year-old girl was excited. She had a penny clutched in her fist that her older sister had given her.

Little Emma had walked the few blocks to the candy store many times before with her sisters. She knew the way. She also knew that she should make sure no trains were approaching on the tracks she had to cross.

Since their mother's death, Emma and her sisters had lived with their father, who worked at the Semet Solvay Coke Co. She skipped along the sidewalk, singing to herself. As she approached the tracks, she saw the gates were down and a train was going by so she waited impatiently for it to pass. After all, she was in quite a hurry to get her candy.

The caboose went by, disappearing down the track. Emma didn't wait for the gates to go up. Now that the train was gone, she could be on her way. She went around the gate and stepped gingerly over the track.

Edward McGrath, 50, was about forty feet away, tending to his duties as agent at the Stowell station. McGrath was a veteran railroad man who, through years of experience, had learned to calculate the speed of a train as it approached. He also knew how long it took an engineer to stop a barreling freight.

McGrath had learned the power and danger of the huge locomotives the hard way. His foot had been crushed years earlier when it got in the way. He walked with a peg attached to the bottom of his leg where his foot once was.

On this lazy August day, McGrath watched Emma as she went around the gate and stepped on to the tracks. But he knew something that Emma didn't: A faster freight than the eastbound train which now had gone out of sight was bearing down on the crossing from the west.

Emma heard the whistle, too, just as she was stepping over the first track. She tensed in surprise, then tripped, sprawling down on the steel on concrete. The oncoming train, pulled by two powerful locomotives, was closer now, less than two blocks away.

In a split second, McGrath sized up the situation. Only one other person besides himself could rescue the little girl. But he was on the other side of the crossing walking away and wasn't aware of Emma's plight.

McGrath ran as best he could toward the girl, dragging his peg leg along behind him. She was crying. Could he make it in time? Or would he make it just far enough for a good view of a terrible tragedy? The train whistle sounded again, much closer now, as McGrath desperately struggled on, trying to reach the small girl, who still hadn't gotten up.

The train was just a few hundred feet down the track when McGrath finally reached the girl. He scooped her up into his arms and quickly fell away from the oncoming train. The huge locomotive brushed their clothing as it rumbled past but, amazingly, Emma and her rescuer escaped unharmed.

"It was the bravest deed I ever saw," said a police officer who witnessed the incident as he, too, was running to help. "When I saw the crippled man jump in front of the locomotive, I thought both the child and the man were doomed."

McGrath, humble after his heroic deed, said he decided to try to rescue the girl so he wouldn't be haunted by her gruesome death.

"It wasn't anything," he told a *Milwaukee Journal* reporter. "I couldn't stand to see a little girl ground to death under the wheels, could I? A man has to take a chance and if that child had died, its screams would have haunted my sleep."

The station agent said his railroad experience helped him realize that he was the girl's only hope.

"Being an old railroad man, I am quite accustomed

to judging distances and acting on the moment and I did it in this case. I measured the distance and managed to escape all right."

McGrath was awarded a bronze medal from the Carnegie Hero Fund Commission and $1,000 to pay off the mortgage on his home.

As for Emma, she turned six just three days after her narrow escape, celebrating a very special birthday.

Chapter 4

Wisconsin angel

Cordelia Perrine Harvey

When Cordelia Perrine married young Louis Harvey in 1847, she couldn't know that she was marrying a future Wisconsin governor. She also couldn't know the heroic role she would play in saving Civil War soldiers.

Cordelia and Louis both were born in New York State but their families emigrated to Kenosha, Wisconsin, then known as Southport. Cordelia, who was said to have a magnetic and frank personality, came to Wisconsin at age 16.

Both were well-educated. Louis worked as a teacher and principal at Southport Academy until 1844, when he became editor of the *Southport American,* a Whig newspaper. He was appointed postmaster by President John Tyler but lost the job when he refused to support all of the President's policies.

After their marriage, the Harveys moved from Kenosha to Clinton, in Rock County, where they opened a general store. Four years later, Louis found a better opportunity to open a flour mill along Turtle Creek at Shopiere. The couple helped build the Shopiere Congregational Church. Their daughter, Mary, was born in 1848 but she died four years later.

Louis Harvey wasn't destined to be just a mill operator. He was soon elected to the state constitutional convention. In 1853, he was elected a Republican state senator from Rock County. He served on the University of Wisconsin Board of Regents, became secretary of state in 1859 and, three years later, with the nation in the throes of the Civil War, Harvey was inaugurated Wisconsin governor.

Not only was Wisconsin's new governor faced with reports of soldiers dying in battle, but Harvey also was told that many wounded soldiers died because of unsanitary conditions, a shortage of medical supplies and the southern climate.

The battle of Shiloh on April 6-7, 1862, took a heavy toll and Harvey decided to make a personal inspection of encampments of Wisconsin soldiers. He headed for southern Illinois, where he visited sick and wounded soldiers at Cairo, Illinois, Mound City, Kentucky and Paducah, Kentucky.

The governor's entourage went farther south, where a freak accident at Savannah, Tennessee brought a tragic end to his inspection. As he was moving from one boat to another on a rainy night, Harvey's foot slipped and he plunged into the river and drowned.

State Historical Society of Wisconsin

Cordelia Harvey

After the funeral, Cordelia Harvey returned to the couple's small white house in Shopiere. Edward Salomon was sworn in as the new Wisconsin governor. But the widow wasn't content to grieve alone. She contacted Salomon and offered to finish the inspection her husband had begun. That fall, the governor made her a Wisconsin sanitary agent and dispatched her to St. Louis.

Cordelia Harvey was shocked at what she found.

Unclean conditions, poorly trained medical staff and the heat contributed to frequent bouts of pneumonia, chronic diarrhea and camp fevers that decimated the wounded soldiers. Of 11,000 Wisconsin soldiers who died during the Civil War, 7,000 died of disease instead of battle wounds.

She inspected hospitals at St. Louis; Cape Girardeau, Missouri; Memphis; Cornith, Mississippi; Jackson, Mississippi; and La Grange, Mississippi. A tall woman, she often wore a black hood that resembled a nun's habit. As Cordelia Harvey moved among the soldiers, she became known as the "Wisconsin Angel" as delirious soldiers saw her as a hooded shadow passing by the sickbeds and begged her to rescue them.

She wrote letters and sought furloughs for many of the sick and dying men until, finally, in 1863, Cordelia Harvey herself fell victim to illness and was forced to return to the North. She recuperated for several months in New York and Wisconsin. Perhaps it was during her convalescence that Cordelia Harvey hit upon a plan she felt could save the lives of thousands of Wisconsin soldiers. If coming North had helped her back to health, it could do the same for them.

Mrs. Harvey carried her crusade to Washington, D.C. Gov. Salomon agreed with her diagnosis that building convalescent hospitals in the North could save many lives. She brought petitions with 8,000 names with her to Washington. The petitions sought federal money to construct hospitals in the North. She got an interview with President Lincoln and placed the petitions on his desk.

She told the President that many more lives would be lost unless sick and wounded soldiers were permitted to travel to the North for their convalescence, taking advantage of the cooler climate and more sanitary conditions.

Lincoln wasn't convinced. He already had rejected a plan to build northern hospitals. Taking sick and wounded soldiers too far away from the battlefront could encourage desertion, he feared.

Dejected, Mrs. Harvey returned to the rooming house where she was staying. But the next morning she was back at the White House and once again confronted the President. She told Lincoln that she planned to stay in Washington until she could convince him of her plan.

Mrs. Harvey told him of her visits to troop encampments, relating shocking details of the poor medical conditions she had found. He told her to return the next day. But that afternoon, Lincoln issued an order to establish military hospitals in the North.

When Mrs. Harvey returned, he told her that the first hospital would be named for her. She suggested it be named for her dead husband instead.

Hospitals were established in Madison, Milwaukee and Prairie du Chien. A three-story octagonal limestone building along Madison's Lake Monona was christened the Harvey United States Army Hospital. More than 630 soldiers were treated there before the war ended. After the war, it was converted to a home for soldiers' orphans.

Mrs. Harvey played a major role in establishing

the orphanage and turned her efforts to helping poor children. She married the Rev. Albert Chester of Buffalo, N.Y. and the couple settled in Clinton, Wisconsin. She died Feb. 27, 1895, and is buried beside her first husband, Louis Harvey, at Forest Hill Cemetery in Madison.

Chapter 5

A record number of kills
Richard Ira Bong

T he pilot gunned the jet engine of the Lockheed
P-80 and headed down the Burbank, Cal. run-
way. A puff of vapor poured from the rear as the plane
lifted off. At a height of about 50 feet, the plane passed
over the airport boundary fence. Suddenly, the engine
cut off. Desperately trying to restart the engine, the
pilot made a right turn over Valhalla Memorial Park.
He tried dipping each wing to keep the craft aloft but
it was no use. The plane passed over high-tension wires
as the altitude slipped to about 30 feet.

Witnesses said they saw an explosion of black
smoke. They watched the pilot as he now tried to
crawl out of the plane, hoping he was high enough for
his parachute to open. The aircraft stalled and plunged
to the ground in a terrific explosion.

The pilot, Richard Ira Bong, died in that crash. It

was ironic that Bong, known as America's ace of aces, didn't die in combat over New Guinea or the Philippines, where he shot down a record 40 Japanese planes. He died testing a new plane with a jet engine over the peaceful skies of California.

It is significant perhaps that Bong died on Aug. 6, 1945, the same day the first atomic bomb was dropped on Hiroshima, leading to the end of World War II. Bong belonged to a different era — an era of fierce air battles in propeller-driven fighters, long before the "smart bombs" of the 1991 Persian Gulf War.

Bong was an unlikely candidate for a record-setting fighter pilot. He was quiet almost to the point of shyness. He was humble and seemed to view his celebrity as a war hero as somewhat of an annoyance. He enjoyed carousing as much as his buddies but in his own laid-back style. He lacked the braggart's brashness of a classic John Wayne war hero.

Bong, born in 1921, was the oldest of nine children, the son of Swedish immigrant Gust Bong, who came to America in 1896 to settle near the logging town of Poplar in the northwest corner of Wisconsin about 40 miles from Superior.

Each of the children was assigned farm chores such as taking care of the cows and hogs or cleaning the barn. Dick Bong also was an avid hunter and fisherman and, for his twelfth birthday, he received a Winchester .22-caliber rifle. He liked to play hockey in the winter and baseball during the summer. As a pitcher, young Dick prided himself on his curve ball.

During the long, cold winters, he often built mod-

els of World War I airplanes. When a plane flew overhead, young Dick — like many boys of his era —
would stop and watch it until it was out of sight.
Although few planes were in the air, he got to watch
more than his share of them in 1928, when they would
fly the mail directly over the Bong farm to President
Calvin Coolidge's summer White House at Superior.

At Superior Central High School, he played the
clarinet in the band and the part of a character named
Pinky in a play. After the play, his classmates dubbed
him with the nickname "Pinky" Bong.

After graduation in 1938, Bong enrolled at the
now defunct Superior State Teachers College, where
his specific interest was engineering. He also enrolled
in the Civilian Pilot Training Program. The program
was started by President Franklin Roosevelt as a way
to strengthen America's military in case it might be
needed to confront the growing menace of the Axis
Powers in Europe and the Pacific.

Dick Bong's first flight was Sept. 24, 1940, in a
Piper J-3 Cub. Within four years, he would set his kill
record. Although he seemed comfortable at the con-
trols of the small training aircraft, Bong's instructors
said he tended to skid on turns and climb too steeply.

In 1941, he was accepted into the aviation cadet
program of the Army Air Corps. He was assigned to
the Rankin Aeronautical Academy at Tulare, Cal., where
his instructor was John Gilbert Rankin, a stunt pilot
known as "Tex."

Later that summer, Bong was sent to Gardner Field
in California for basic training. A few months later, he

went on to Luke Field at Phoenix, Arizona, where one of his instructors was Barry Goldwater. Goldwater, the longtime Arizona senator and 1964 presidential candidate, was supposed to play golf with Bong on the day he died.

The Japanese bombing of Pearl Harbor on Dec. 7, 1941, put America's war preparations on a fast track. With his pilot training completed, Bong reported in May 1942 to the 49th Pursuit Squadron at Hamilton Field in San Francisco, The squadron was supposed to be sent to North Africa. After training in slower AT-6 aircraft, Bong finally got to fly a P-38 fighter. It was this plane, also known as the Lightning, in which he would set his record.

Before the squadron headed overseas, Bong and another pilot became involved in what was dubbed the Golden Gate incident. According to an account by Bong's brother, Carl, in the book *Ace of Aces,* another pilot flew under the Golden Gate Bridge while Dick Bong buzzed a house, flying a few feet above the roof. In other accounts, Dick Bong is credited with flying under the bridge. In any case, both pilots were booted out of the 49th Squadron and grounded for six weeks. That twist of fate, however, meant Bong would go to the South Pacific instead.

Bong and several other pilots flew in September 1942 to Australia, where they were assigned to the 39th Squadron at Schwimmer Air Base on the coast of New Guinea. On Dec. 27, Bong shot down his first enemy aircraft, a Japanese Zero fighter. He and 11 other pilots were scrambled to head off an incoming raid. Bong quickly got into the thick of the air battle, firing at a couple of targets and missing. With an enemy plane on his tail, Bong dived and came face-to-face with a bomber. He fired first and the Japanese plane went down. He turned and came upon a Zero. Firing again, he got his second kill within a few minutes.

Bong was awarded a Silver Star for the two kills in that action. He still was a long way from his 40-kill record. But he would down three more enemy planes during missions in early January. His fifth downed plane earned him the Distinguished Flying Cross.

Bong never considered himself a very good shot. His success in aerial combat was due more to his ability to maneuver the aircraft, perhaps using tactics he first learned from stunt pilot Tex Rankin. He was adept at getting on the tail of an enemy plane and pursuing mercilessly until he got off a fatal shot. Despite his quiet manner, Bong also wasn't timid about taking risks and getting into the midst of the fighting.

After some leave time in Australia, Bong returned to New Guinea, reporting to the 9th Squadron. In February, he fought in the Bismarck Sea Battle and, on March 11, Bong came close to losing his life, when he was pursued by nine Japanese Zeros. Once again, his masterful tactics at diving and turning helped him escape. By the end of March, Bong had nine confirmed kills and several probables, which don't count in his record.

By late July, the Allies had gained the upper hand over the Japanese in New Guinea but there still were

State Historical Society of Wisconsin

Richard Bong, center, returns home for a visit.

plenty of battles to be fought. On July 26, Bong and his squadron were on patrol over the Markham Valley when he spotted about 20 Japanese fighters. He dove and confronted one plane head-on, watching as the enemy aircraft burst into flames. From a 45-degree angle, he shot at another plane and saw pieces of the fuselage blow off. A third round from his gun sent another plane bursting into flames and a fourth burst knocked off engine pieces of yet another plane.

These four enemy kills in a single mission boosted Bong's total to 15 and earned him the Distinguished Service Cross. Bong described the scene to reporters:

"Things happened so fast that all I can recall is the sky being full of Japanese planes twisting crazily, hot lead whizzing past my face and all hell breaking loose above and below me."

Another kill two days later brought Bong within 10 of World War I ace Eddie Rickenbacker's record 26 kills and the media began to take notice. The next couple of months were relatively quiet for the northern Wisconsin pilot until October, when more skirmishes raised his total to 19. He now was three kills ahead of his nearest competitor and seven away from Rickenbacker's record. In letters home, Bong wrote that life on the remote air base was no picnic and he missed eating chicken, venison and apple pie, as well as deer hunting.

By the fall, he had downed 21 Japanese aircraft. So far, Bong had come through all of this action without a scratch. On a couple of occasions, his plane was damaged and, in early November, two of his wingmen, flying in formation adjacent to him, were lost in action on November 5 and again on November 7. Critics said Bong was thinking too much about his own score and wasn't providing enough protection for other members of his squadron. In the heat of a dogfight, it was just as difficult for American pilots to stay with Bong as it was for the enemy to stay away. And some of the criticism probably stemmed from jealousy over Bong's mounting kill scorecard.

By mid-November, Bong was on his way home to Poplar for a much-deserved leave. Newspaper reporters and photographers flocked to the Bong farm to chronicle the homecoming of a war hero. Contingents from the American Legion, Superior State Teachers

College and the R.O.T.C. band also participated in the welcome.

After a night's rest, Dick went deer hunting with his two brothers, Carl and Roy. Although both brothers got their deer, Dick was less successful than he'd been against the Japanese. To satisfy the news media, however, the brothers credited their kills to their famous brother.

Bong told reporters he "would rather shoot deer" than Japanese planes but that shooting a deer bothered him more because knocking out a plane "is completely impersonal."

A parade was held in his honor and Superior declared "Dick Bong Day." The event that would prove most significant, however, was that Bong was asked to crown the homecoming king and queen at the college. He met the outgoing queen, Marge Vattendahl, and they began dating.

In mid-December, Bong went to Washington, D.C., where he appeared in newsreels and hobnobbed with politicians. In late January, most residents of Poplar turned out to wish him well as Bong departed for the war zone.

By this time, however, Bong had become a valuable property. Instead of going back into combat, he was assigned to Air Force command headquarters. He was, however, allowed to fly free-lance missions with Tom Lynch, another pilot assigned to headquarters.

Bong and Lynch notched up a string of kills, moving Bong closer to the Rickenbacker record. On March 8, however, Lynch was shot down and killed.

By the end of the month, Bong had 25 confirmed kills. He also had decided to ask Marge Vattendahl to marry him. For good luck, he painted her picture on a P-38 along with rows of Japanese flags designating his kills. But that plane proved ill-fated and was lost while being flown by another pilot.

On April 12, 1944, Bong shot down two Japanese Oscars, raising his score to 27 and breaking the Rickenbacker record. Congratulations came from across the globe. Rickenbacker and Gen. Douglas MacArthur, also a Wisconsin hero, both sent wires to the Wisconsin farm boy turned pilot. Worst of all for Bong, he was barred from further combat flying and, on May 3, he was ordered back home.

His first stop was Washington, D.C., where Bong met Pentagon officials. The next order of business was proposing to Marge and he gave her a diamond engagement ring on June 1. By September, he was back in New Guinea.

Bong now achieved the status of combat flight instructor and was ordered not to shoot except in self-defense. The Air Force didn't want to lose one of its biggest walking advertisements for war bonds.

But Bong seemed to come across quite a few self-defense situations and his kill total continued to climb. By Nov. 11, he had downed a phenomenal total of 36 Japanese planes.

Bong was cited by his commander, Gen. George Kenney, for "conspicuous gallantry and intrepidity in action." On Dec. 12, Bong was awarded the Congressional Medal of Honor by Gen. MacArthur.

Pressure mounted on Kenney to send him home before he got killed. Kenney decided privately that Bong would be forced to quit when the total reached forty. He got it on Dec. 17, five days after receiving the nation's highest honor. During the three previous months, he had downed a dozen Japanese planes while serving as a flight instructor and inspecting the gunnery of various units.

On Feb. 10, 1945, Dick and Marge were married in an evening ceremony at Concordia Lutheran Church in Superior while a bevy of reporters swarmed outside. The honeymoon began at the Hotel Nicolet in Minneapolis and the couple went on to southern California.

The Hollywood studios courted Bong, eager to win the rights to his amazing story. Bong was assigned to Lockheed's plant in Burbank, where he would help test Lockheed's new P-80 jet aircraft. Several test planes already had been lost and, several months later, Bong would become another of those statistics.

A bronze head honoring Bong was presented a year later to the Wisconsin State Historical Society. Marge Bong landed a job in Hollywood as a model and said she was going to pursue a movie career. In October 1946, she married James Baird, the sales manager of a textile importing firm in Beverly Hills.

Forty years after the fatal crash, test pilot Chuck Yeager criticized Bong in a biography published in the mid-1980s. Yeager, the first pilot to break the sound barrier in 1947, said he had witnessed Bong's crash.

"Arrogance got more pilots in trouble than faulty equipment," Yeager wrote. "That's what killed Dick Bong, our top war ace in the Pacific."

Yeager said Bong got swept up in Hollywood society and didn't spend enough time learning the intricacies of the new jet engines. Crash records indicate Bong may have failed to turn on an auxiliary fuel pump that may have saved his life. Superior residents were outraged at Yeager's derogatory comments about their war hero and demanded he come to Superior to explain them but Yeager refused.

Wisconsin and its residents have honored Bong in various ways, naming a state forest, streets and a bridge connecting Superior and Duluth after him.

Although Yeager's comments seemed a bit harsh, it seems clear that Bong belonged to a different era — an era that preceded jet engines, atomic weapons and smart bombs. The record number of enemy planes he shot down probably will stand forever because they just don't fight that way anymore.

Chapter 6

Temperance brings strength
Frances Willard

F rances Willard is mostly remembered as president of the Women's Christian Temperance Union, an organization not taken seriously since the fall of Prohibition.

But she also was a noted educator, a supporter of women's right to vote and an ancestor of today's feminists. She fought for prison reform, abolishing slavery, establishing social welfare services, expanding public education and eliminating child labor.

Although the state of Illinois, where she spent much of her adult life, honored her by commissioning a statue in the U.S. Capitol, her Wisconsin upbringing clearly contributed to her success.

She was born in Churchville, N.Y. on Sept. 28, 1839. Her mother had been a teacher and her father was a storekeeper and part-time minister. Her brother,

Oliver, feared young Frances would die because the family had lost an infant girl a year earlier. But Frances proved not only to be a healthy child but a precocious one, learning to talk before she could walk. When she was two, the Willard family moved to Oberlin, Ohio, then to a farm near Janesville, Wisconsin in 1846. The Willard property, known as Forest Home, grew into one of Wisconsin's most productive farms.

As a girl, Frances Willard was a tomboy. She once rode a cow after her father forbade her from riding horses, an escapade that persuaded her father to relent. She want to be called "Frank" because, she said, she "preferred a boy's name and a boy's carefree lifestyle."

Male and female roles were not clearly defined in the Willard family. Frances didn't learn to cook or sew until she was a teenager. Her mother, Mary, was a teacher for eleven years prior to her marriage and she tutored her Frances and her sister, also named Mary.

When she left home to attend North-Western Female College in Evanston, Frances Willard brought her unusual view of the world with her. She was shy and more interested in academics than men. After college, she taught school in River Forest and Kankakee, Illinois. She became engaged to marry Charles Fowler, a Methodist minister, but returned his ring in early 1862. She had one other relationship four years later but never married.

A month after Frances broke off the relationship with Fowler, her sister died of consumption. In 1863, she wrote and had published a book about her sister titled *Nineteen Beautiful Years.*

Her first public service came in 1865, when she became corresponding secretary for the American Methodist Centenary Association, which was raising money to build an addition to Garrett Theological Seminary in Evanston. In 1866, she became a teacher at Genesee Wesleyan Seminary in Lima, New York.

After a two-year world tour with a colleague, Kate Jackson, Frances Willard returned to accept the presidency of Evanston College for Ladies, replacing a stringent set of rules for women students with an honor system and becoming an instructor of men's classes at Northwestern as well.

But male students didn't take kindly to a woman instructor of composition. They decorated her blackboard with graffiti and imprisoned a cat in her desk drawer. Fowler, her former fiance, became university president and, after a merger of the college for ladies with the university, stripped her of authority, finally forcing her resignation in 1874.

By 1874, the temperance movement was taking hold in America as women were organizing to seek bans on liquor sales and saloon closures. It may be difficult for us to understand today the prevailing attitudes of the time. The failure of Prohibition may color our historic view of the temperance movement.

In *Frances Willard,* biographer Ruth Bordin writes: "Drink was one great enemy. Americans had wrestled with the personal and social dislocation produced by their society's tendency toward excessive use of alcohol for over half a century when Willard adopted it as her cause.... All through the nineteenth century Americans were heavy users of alcohol, heavier users than they have ever been since."

Willard attended the Women's Congress in October 1873 in New York and presented a paper titled *New Departures in Education.* The congress, the beginnings of a campaign for women's suffrage, convened to organize a group called the Association for the Advancement of Women. She was elected vice president for Illinois. She also made contacts in the temperance cause and, instead of seeking another teaching job, she became a lecturer and organizer for the Chicago chapter of the fledgling Women's Christian Temperance Union.

After serving as national correspondence secretary, Willard challenged national president Annie Wittenmyer and won in 1879. In Boston, she also met Annie Gordon, who would become her lifelong companion. Gordon later served as president of the temperance union before and during Prohibition.

During the 1880s, Willard saw a parallel between the separate movements for temperance and women's suffrage. Her annual convention speeches were widely reported and she became a popular national figure. A speech with a "do everything" theme emphasized using every tactic to work for temperance but also alluded to the fact that women should organize to tackle other issues as well.

In 1883, she foresaw an emancipation of women from domestic chores, imagining meals delivered from a central kitchen by pneumatic tubes and houses heated

Madison Newspapers Inc. newsroom library

Frances Willard

by central gas and water supplied by public reservoir.

Willard also spoke against exploitation of women: "When we reflect — that in Massachusetts and Vermont it is a greater crime to steal a cow than to abduct and ruin a girl, and that in Illinois seduction is not recognized as a crime, it is a marvel not to be explained, that we go the even tenor of our way, too delicate, too refined, too prudish to make any allusion to these awful facts..."

After her mother's death in 1892, Willard joined Lady Henry Somerset in England and the two women worked to bring the temperance movement to a worldwide scale. But Willard, now in her mid-fifties, began to suffer ill health, which was aggravated by her regular trips across the ocean between America and England. In 1895, Willard and Somerset got involved in lobbying the British and American governments to intervene in the wholesale slaughter of Armenian Christians by Turkish soldiers.

Frances Willard died on Feb. 17, 1898, in a New York City hotel room. She had asked that her body be cremated, which at the time was considered a defiant act in itself. Biographer Ruth Bodin writes that Willard was the most popular and famous woman of the nineteenth century and Chicagoans mourned her death:

"The flags of the nation's second largest city floated at half mast. Throngs of silent Chicagoans, thirty thousand in one day, filed by the bier for a parting look at their city's most famous citizen."

In the context of feminism today, Willard may seem somewhat out of date. But the temperance movement provided a catalyst for women to organize and was an important precursor to the suffrage movement and other critical social changes of the early twentieth century.

Chapter 7

His eyes on the skies

Donald "Deke" Slayton

R ichard Bong wasn't the only Wisconsin farm boy who used to gaze skyward whenever an airplane flew overhead. A rural Sparta lad was destined to fly faster and farther than Bong ever dreamed.

Instead of working out in the field, Donald "Deke" Slayton would watch the sky in hopes of spotting an airplane. He was the third in a family of seven children. His father's first wife died when their son, Elwood, was born and Donald, born March 1, 1924, was the first child of his father's second marriage.

Donald's grade-point average at Leon Elementary School and Sparta High School were far above average. He was a quiet boy, later described as intelligent, inquisitive and determined. He liked building airplane models and took a special interest in a high school aeronautical instruction course.

For years, the Slayton farm didn't have electricity and Donald helped milk cows by hand before and after school. He participated in boxing and track and played trumpet in the school band. At the State Fair, he exhibited a pair of Oxford sheep. He would stay in shape by running the mile-and-a-half from the Slayton farm into the village of Leon. He also was a member of the Future Farmers of America.

Farming clearly wasn't in Donald's future. Less than a month before he graduated from high school in June 1942, Donald turned eighteen and he immediately enlisted in the Air Force. His high school diploma was forwarded to him in San Antonio, Texas, where he already was in training as a pilot at Lackland Air Force Base. While Bong was racking up kills in the South Pacific, Slayton was just learning to fly.

After advanced pilot training, Slayton was sent to the Italian theater, where he flew B-25 bombers on 56 missions. He later flew missions over Okinawa and, after four-and-a-half years in the Air Force, he was discharged.

In August 1949, Slayton received a degree in aeronautical engineering at the University of Minnesota and went to work as an engineer for Boeing Aircraft Corp. in Seattle. It was the first time but not the last that Slayton would feel impatient about not being in the pilot's seat. It wasn't the last time he couldn't stand being grounded. He enlisted again in the Air Force in 1951 and was sent to Germany.

In Germany, Slayton fell in love and married Marjorie Lunney of Los Angeles, an Air Force secretary. The couple returned to the United States in July 1955, two months after the wedding. Slayton's returned was well-timed. America's space program was about to be launched and a competition with the Soviets was under way over who would be first to send a man into space.

The desire to beat the Soviets into space was so intense that it reached all the way down into America's grade schools, prompting adoption of more intensive science curricula. The Soviets launched Sputnik but the United States was close on its heels with unmanned launches of its own. The real prize, however, was the first man in space. From its best and brightest pilots, America selected seven men the nation dubbed astronauts. They would be the nation's space pioneers and Donald Slayton, the farm boy from Sparta, was one of them.

"I'd give my left arm to be the first man in space," Slayton said at the time, echoing how they all felt.

These seven men were instant celebrities but the Soviets won the race as Yuri Gagarin became the first man in space. Alan Shepard was chosen as the first American spaceman. After Shepard came Virgil "Gus" Grissom; then John Glenn became the first American to orbit the earth.

In this era before worldwide access through satellite television, Americans followed television and radio reports of Glenn's flight carefully as he circled the globe three times. Slayton would be next. He was selected in late 1961 to follow Glenn on the second American orbital flight. Along the way, Slayton had earned the nickname "Deke." Based on his initials "D.K.", the nickname was to distinguish him from another space program employee named Donald.

Back home in Sparta, Slayton's family was excited about their son's adventure. They had learned to accept his hazardous duty in World War II and, later, as an Air Force jet test pilot.

"We're just living one day at a time," said his mother, Victoria. "We don't know what the future holds for us."

In February 1962, Slayton sat in on debriefing sessions when Glenn plunged back to earth. "Everything he learned will be a help for the next flight," Slayton said. "Actually, John showed us there are some basic things we don't have to worry about — getting sick from the weightless environment and having to take over control of the spaceship — and this takes the limits off a lot of things we can do in future flights."

Slayton clearly was anxious to orbit himself. But it wasn't to be. In March, a physical exam disclosed a persistent heart flutter and a disappointed Slayton was grounded once again. He was replaced by Scott Carpenter for the May 24 flight. In June, another exam eliminated him from all future solo space flights. Over the next several years, Slayton remained a crucial member of America's space team but behind the scenes, helping the other astronauts with operational planning.

"Naturally, I am greatly disappointed," Slayton said. "For more than three years, I have been training and looking forward to an early flight assignment. But I am ready to do whatever is needed. I'll work wherever management feels I can best contribute to the program."

Much later, Slayton would admit that his disappointment was much deeper than his official remarks would imply. In Sparta, his parents were sorry their son was scrubbed but they also were relieved. Mrs. Slayton once called the day her son was selected as one of America's first seven astronauts "my worst day."

Madison Newspapers Inc. newsroom library
Donald "Deke" Slayton

Project Mercury gave way to Project Gemini and then to Apollo and, in 1969, American astronauts became the first men to walk on the moon. Slayton remained grounded. He had resigned his Air Force commission, hoping he might pass a less rigorous civilian physical exam. He was named assistant director for flight crew operations.

Slayton's less glamorous status made him no less of a hero in Wisconsin. He visited his home state frequently, sometimes with James Lovell, the astronaut from Milwaukee. He often toured schools and spoke to civic groups around the state.

In 1970, the Cold War fueled for more than a decade by intense competition in space thawed just a little. Officials of the National Aeronautics and Space Administration went to Moscow to meet with officials of the Soviet Academy of Sciences about a mission in which spacecraft of the two nations could be linked in space with a docking module. Two years later, President Richard Nixon and Soviet Premier Aleksei Kosygin signed the formal Apollo-Soyuz agreement.

As mysteriously as it had emerged, Slayton's heart flutter suddenly disappeared. He was approaching age 50 by now and was about to become America's oldest astronaut. Along with Thomas Stafford and Vance Brand, Slayton was selected to pilot the American half of the Apollo-Soyuz mission in July 1975. Slayton had studied Russian in hopes of landing the assignment.

Soviet cosmonauts Aleksei Leonov and Valery Kubasov lifted from a launching pad in central Russia on July 15. Seven-and-a-half hours later, the American astronauts were launched from Cape Canaveral, Florida. The two spacecrafts met high above the atmosphere two days later.

The spacecrafts docked twice, performed four crew exchanges and conducted 27 scientific experiments. The astronauts and cosmonauts shared meals and held a television news conference before parting on July 19.

Splashdown of the Apollo spacecraft was marred by the accidental release of nitrogen tetroxide gas into the chamber. The astronauts were hospitalized as a precaution and a lung lesion was found in Slayton that doctors said apparently existed before the flight. The lesion was surgically removed and found to be non-cancerous.

But it was too late to scrub Slayton now, as he already had completed a successful mission. It was a mission he had awaited for 16 years since his selection in 1959 as one of the original seven astronauts.

"For some people, life begins at forty," Slayton said. "For me, it's going to be more like fifty-plus."

By the mid-1980s, Slayton still made trips back to Wisconsin, urging young people to take an interest in the space program despite government cutbacks. His trademark crewcut had grown out and his squared-off jaw had grown fleshier. He was the mission director for the private launch of the Conestoga I satellite in 1982 after his job was eliminated by NASA. The times clearly had changed.

Slayton was the last of the original seven to leave the space agency. Shepard became a real estate developer in Houston. Virgil "Gus" Grissom died in an Apollo launching pad fire in January 1967. John Glenn became a U.S. senator from Ohio. Scott Carpenter, Walter Schirra and L. Gordon Cooper turned to business and consulting.

By the late 1980s, Slayton was still promoting more space projects. He suggested the United States and Soviet Union set aside political differences and join together for a mission to Mars. He joined a company that planned to pioneer the launching of cremated bodies into orbit. Before he died of cancer in 1993, Slayton wrote a book and hosted a television documentary about his career in the space program.

To the very end, Slayton never lost the spirit of that Sparta farm boy who gazed into the sky in awe.

Chapter 8

A woman leads the way

Margaret Brennecke

Unlike a treacherous saltwater sound or raging ocean tide, Madison's Lake Mendota normally is a peaceful body of water. One of the best times of the year in Wisconsin's capital city is spring, after the snow and ice melt and the long, cold winter warms away.

Due to the length and severity of Wisconsin winters, there is a temptation to rush the season. Such was the case on April 24, 1921. It was one of those sunny, brisk days of spring: warm but with a stiff wind that formed whitecaps on the usually placid lake.

Two University of Wisconsin students, Esther Wepking and Arthur Harwood, thought it was a perfect day for canoeing on the lake. They had paddled several feet off Picnic Point near the campus when their canoe was hit by a towering wave and it capsized. The two students clung desperately to the overturned canoe, hoping for a quick rescue from the cold water. No other boaters, however, were nearby. For more than an hour, Wepking and Harwood clung to their canoe, trying to stay conscious now, as the water numbed their bodies.

On Picnic Point, several other students were enjoying the balmy weather. They noticed the capsized canoe and reported it to authorities but weren't about to risk their own lives by venturing into the rough water and two-foot waves. Except for Margaret Brennecke, that is.

Brennecke, a freshman from Aurora, Ill., jumped in a canoe with another student, Edward Haugen, and they began paddling toward Wepking and Harwood, who by now were bobbing in and out of the water. Not about to be outdone by a woman, several of the reluctant men on the point now also got into canoes and headed for the stranded students.

Brennecke paddled for a half mile before she reached the overturned canoe. She saw that Wepking had nearly lost consciousness. With help from men in two other canoes, Brennecke pulled the woman from the water just as she also was losing her hold on the capsized canoe. One of the men stripped off his shirt and tied the three canoes together for stability among the waves. Brennecke lay Wepking across the three canoes and began resuscitation efforts. Harwood was pulled by the men from the frigid water but he hadn't lost consciousness.

Slowly, while the waves continued to shower them and batter the makeshift raft, Brennecke saw Wepking open her eyes. Wepking coughed and clung tightly to one of the men while Brennecke worked quickly to get the remaining water out of her lungs.

Brennecke and the other rescuers now turned their efforts to getting the makeshift raft to shore. With the canoes lashed together, they had little control and drifted with the waves. They tried to paddle to the opposite shore, more than a mile away, but soon were pounded by five-foot waves, whipped by the wind.

Suddenly, a huge wave swept across the raft and it proved too much for the weakened Wepking. She lost her grip and in an instant was swept under, never to be seen alive again. Everett Patten, one of the rescuers, dived into the water but Wepking was gone.

One of the canoes was rapidly filling with water and, for a while, it looked as though the lake would claim its victims after all. Soon the raft capsized, spilling the rescuers into the water. Harwood grabbed a life preserver and floated away. Brennecke and two men grabbed other life preservers and swam toward shore.

It was then that Alex Lamont, another student, reached them in a small rowboat. After swimming about a thousand feet, Brennecke was taken into the boat and they again headed for shore. Before they reached shore, Lamont's boat swamped, but a speedboat arrived and took Lamont, Harwood and the rescuers aboard.

"Had it not been for Lamont, it is probable that the lake would have claimed the other five," a fire official said later.

One rescuer, Howell Smith, was semi-conscious when he was pulled from the water. Patten swam about thirty feet when he spotted the speedboat so he returned to the raft. When the speedboat reached the raft, only Haugen's hand was visible above the water as he held on. Haugen, who was pulled out in a dazed condition, likely would have drowned if the boat had taken a few minutes more. James Studley, a forest products engineer and a poor swimmer, also was rescued clinging to the raft next to Haugen. Sidney Bentley swam to shallow water before he collapsed and was carried the rest of the way.

Brennecke received a bronze medal and $500 from the Carnegie Hero Fund Commission for her part in the rescue. Haugen, Studley, Smith, Bentley and Patten also received bronze medals and $500 from the commission.

But the hero of the day clearly was Brennecke, a woman who refused to follow the timidity of the men around her — instead, striking out on her own in a valiant attempt to rescue the stranded couple.

"I'd certainly like to get to know that plucky girl who went out with us," Patten said after the ordeal. "She certainly was brave."

Chapter 9

A dog to the rescue
Ezekiel Von Swashbuckler

Oscar Muench couldn't understand why his dog, I-Zeke, wasn't following his normal routine that Saturday night — February 12, 1994. Usually, Muench would let out the German shepherd about 10:30 p.m., put on some coffee and let him back in. This time, I-Zeke wanted to stay downstairs with Muench's 80-year-old mother, Molly Spaun.

"I don't know what possessed him to do that but he did," Muench said.

Molly Spaun is often called the first lady of Superior's tavern business. She and her husband opened Molly's Tavern in 1938 and she's operated the establishment at its current location in the city's North End since 1952.

I-Zeke wasn't named after a World War II Japanese fighter plane. I-Zeke is short for Ezekiel Von

Swashbuckler. Muench pronounced the name "I-Zekiel" and I-Zeke for short.

The dog wasn't his first choice when he and his mother brought the four-month-old pup home from Hermantown, Minnesota eight years ago. But another family who adopted him took him back because they didn't like him.

"There was a dog I liked better than him — but he (I-Zeke) was spunkier," Muench said.

He wanted a spunky dog who could hold his own with Cynthia J. June, a German shepherd they already owned. I-Zeke turned out not only to be spunky but a genuine lifesaver.

About 6:30 a.m. on Feb. 13, I-Zeke, who happened to be in the right place at the right time, jumped on Molly Spaun's bed and awakened her.

"The room was full of smoke," she said later. "I thought I was dreaming. Then I heard some crackling. I looked toward the next room and saw a bright light."

Molly's Tavern was on fire. She screamed to a bartender who was staying in an apartment next to hers and both fled outside with the dog. Besides saving Molly's life, I-Zeke's quick action also meant the fire was reported quickly and damage was confined to a bathroom and Spaun's apartment.

The fire occurred two days before Molly Spaun's 80th birthday so the party was moved to a nearby tavern called Lost in the 50's. I-Zeke wasn't invited but he was rewarded with lamb chops, one of his favorite foods.

Muench said he wouldn't be surprised if the dog sensed something was wrong that night and, for that reason, he stayed downstairs with his mother.

"We just take him for granted," he said. "You relate to him like you would to a five- or six-year-old child."

I-Zeke marked his eighth birthday on May 30, 1995, and Muench said most of the fire damage has been repaired. And thanks to the dog, Molly Spaun still operates her tavern that way she has for nearly sixty years.

Chapter 10

The progressive tradition
Belle and Robert M. La Follette

Seventy years after his death in 1925, Robert Marion La Follette Sr. and his wife, Belle Case La Follette, remain Wisconsin's most beloved political figures. Throughout his career as a lawyer, politician, governor and U.S. senator, "Fighting Bob" La Follette left a legacy that no other politician has matched or likely ever will. His progressive stamp on state and national politics lingers even today. Belle La Follette was more than merely a help-mate. Through her involvement in *La Follette's Weekly* and social causes, she wielded her own political influence.

The La Follette family, of French Huguenot ancestry, came to Wisconsin in 1850 from Virginia, Kentucky. Born on June 14, 1855, Robert La Follette grew up on a farm in the Dane County town of Primrose, southwest of Madison. He was the youngest of

Madison Newspapers Inc. newsroom library

Robert M. LaFollette

four children and his father died when he was six months old.

For a while, Robert's mother stayed on the farm but eventually remarried and moved to Argyle, in Green County, where Robert attended public school. He may have begun his career in public speaking at the Argyle barbershop, where he often debated issues of the day with the customers.

Although he never attended high school, Robert was accepted by the preparatory department of the University of Wisconsin. His family moved with him to Madison, where they rented a home on Spring Street, then at the outskirts of the city. His mother ran a student boarding house and the family kept a cow and horse. Robert rode the horse back and forth to his job as a teacher at a country school near Madison.

Belle Case La Follette was born April 21, 1859, in Juneau County, Wisconsin to Arson and Mary Nesbitt Case. She grew up on a farm near Baraboo and attended the University of Wisconsin in 1875, where she proved to be an outstanding student.

In 1879, Robert La Follette gained his first notoriety by winning the Northern Oratorical League's prize for a scholarly lecture about Shakespeare's character Iago. He described Iago has having "the cold passion of intellect, whose icy touch chills the warm life in all its reaches." La Follette was celebrated as a hero in Madison for winning the contest and he considered becoming an actor. But Lawrence Barrett, a prominent actor of the time, told the young man he probably was too short for the stage.

Instead, young La Follette studied law and he began a practice in Madison in 1880. But the private practice was short-lived, for he was soon elected Dane County district attorney. La Follette won election that year against the opposition of Elisha W. Keyes, Madison postmaster and a political boss of the time.

Belle Case also was honored for her oratory. She won the Lewis Prize for her address at the university commencement in 1879. She met Robert La Follette while both were in law school.

They were married in 1881. Belle Case La Follette, the first woman to receive a law degree from the University of Wisconsin Law School, was much more than a mother and wife. Trained in the law, she became La Follette's chief counsel throughout many of his campaigns. She worked hard for women's suffrage and fought for women's rights. She also opposed slavery and supported expansion of civil rights.

After two terms as district attorney, La Follette, a Republican, was elected to Congress, at age 29, the youngest member that year. By the time of his third term, La Follette had gained a seat on the House Ways and Means Committee.

He was defeated in 1890 after clashing with state Sen. Philetus Sawyer of Oshkosh over a bill that La Follette feared would promote the plundering of Indian lands. When Sawyer tried to get La Follette to fix a court case involving Sawyer's brother-in-law, La Follette was outraged and vowed to clean up politics in the state.

Following the Sawyer incident, La Follette began a crusade to capture the governor's chair. Viewed as a traitor to the cause, he organized a major revolt in Republican ranks, campaigning on a platform that called for giving political power back to the citizens instead of the political bosses. He insisted the railroads should pay their fair share of property taxes. In the elections of 1894 and 1896, La Follette's reform forces failed. But in 1900, he was elected governor — the first Wisconsin governor born in the state.

With his election, La Follette's battleground shifted to the Legislature, which opposed his efforts to approve primary election legislation and a fairer system for taxing the railroads. But an opportunity to use his powerful public speaking ability and take his case to the people came in the form of a minor bill to tax farmer's dogs. He blasted the Legislature for trying to

Madison newspapers Inc. newsroom library

Belle Case La Follette

tax dogs that protected farm homes while letting railroad barons avoid millions of dollars in taxes.

Touring county fairs in 1901 and 1902, La Follette continued his campaign against the Legislature. His speeches were entertaining as he mimicked his opponents. When he was re-elected governor in 1902, voters also sent some sympathetic legislators with him to the Capitol. Railroad and inheritance taxes were enacted, along with the primary election law.

Stalwart Republicans, boosted by railroad lobbyists, tried to oust La Follette from the ticket in 1904 but La Follette was nominated at the famous "Gymnasium Convention," where the stalwart faction defected when they realized they couldn't prevent his nomination. He was re-elected, along with reform-minded legislators.

A railroad commission was established, the state civil service law was passed and a forest conservation program was established. La Follette's frequent use of university professors on state boards and commissions became part of the "Wisconsin Idea" and was widely copied in other states.

In 1905, before U.S. senators were elected by popular vote, the Legislature nominated him to the post and La Follette took his reform platform to the national arena. His Wisconsin reputation, however, prompted the Republican congressional leadership to assign him a seat away from them. He was assigned to the minor Committee on the Potomac Front and the Committee on Indian Affairs, which they also thought would keep him out of trouble. They were wrong.

He began to battle efforts by coal and oil companies to take over Indian lands. Although those efforts aggravated the political leadership, they inspired others. The La Follettes started their own magazine, *La Follette's Weekly*, in 1909 to boost reform efforts. Belle wrote articles supporting child labor laws, better working conditions for mothers and improved race relations. She once went directly to President Woodrow Wilson to protest a plan to reimpose segregation in the federal Bureau of Engraving and Printing.

Opponents saw an opportunity to defeat him in 1910, when La Follette became ill and couldn't campaign for re-election. Rail and oil money poured into the state to support his demise. But U.S. Senate colleagues also came to campaign on his behalf and La Follette was re-elected.

Against the odds, La Follette managed to fight for federal laws initiating government valuation of railroads, regulating telegraph and telephone rates, setting an eight-hour work day for government employees, establishing the parcel post system, enacting the federal income tax, appointing a tariff commission, abolishing injunctions in labor disputes and imposing taxes on war profits.

In 1912, he mounted a campaign for President but former President Theodore Roosevelt destroyed La Follette's campaign when he entered the race as a third-party candidate. Roosevelt's campaign also assured the defeat of Republican William Howard Taft and the election of Wilson.

In 1913, Belle La Follette appeared before the U.S.

Senate Committee on Woman Suffrage, supporting a constitutional amendment to give the women the right to vote.

Robert La Follette's propensity to go against the grain surfaced again in 1919, when he voted against entry of the United States into World War I. He was denounced as a German sympathizer and University of Wisconsin students hanged him in effigy. He was expelled from the prestigious Madison Club and a senate committee was appointed to investigate his conduct.

"War is a terribly destructive force, even beyond the limits of the battle front and the war zones," he wrote to a friend. "Its influence involves the whole community. It warps men's judgment, distorts the true standard of patriotism, breeds distrust and suspicion among neighbors, inflames passions, encourages violence, develops abuse of power, tyrannizes over men and women, even in the purely social relations of life, and terrifies whole communities into the most abject surrender of every right which is the heritage of free government."

Despite the ferocity of the outcry against him, the war's quick resolution cooled passions and, in 1922, he was re-elected to the Senate. In one of his most famous muckraking efforts, La Follette drafted a resolution that launched an investigation into the Teapot Dome affair, a major oil scandal during the Harding administration which resulted in a prison term for the Secretary of the Interior and resignation of the Secretary of the Navy.

In 1924, La Follette again announced his candidacy for President on a third-party ticket. His platform called for disarmament, government ownership of railroads, farm relief and labor reform. He raised $225,000 for the campaign through small donations at his stump speeches. He refused to accept the support of the Communists and denounced the Ku Klux Klan. But he won only Wisconsin's 13 electoral votes in the election and garnered about 4.8 million votes.

That gruelling campaign was to be La Follette's last hurrah. He died in Washington, D.C. on June 18, 1925, of a heart ailment. A train took La Follette's body back to Madison and railroad workers lined the tracks in some places, mourning the man who had championed better working conditions for them. In Madison, thousands lined the streets as the hearse left the Capitol for La Follette's final resting place at Forest Hill Cemetery.

Belle Case La Follette served as her husband's valuable counsel until the end. Lincoln Steffens, a muckraking journalist of the early 20th Century, called her "the woman triumphant" who had "a funny little chuckling laugh which she laughed when a word or an act fixed a fact." She declined offers to run for Robert's senate seat, then watched as her sons sought public office.

In 1929, a statue of Robert La Follette was erected in the Capitol's Hall of Fame. But La Follette's true legacy came through his sons Robert Jr. and Philip, both of whom entered public service. Robert Jr. was elected in 1925 to fill out his father's Senate term. He supported Franklin Roosevelt and helped draft unemployment relief, labor and tax reform legislation. Although he lacked his father's speaking abilities, Robert Jr. was re-elected three times until his defeat in 1946 by Joseph McCarthy. McCarthy, later notorious for his blistering anti-Communist crusades, won by fewer than 5,000 votes after Robert Jr. spent too much time pushing a congressional reform act instead of campaigning.

Like his father, Philip La Follette served as Dane County district attorney and, later, Wisconsin governor. In 1934, he and Robert Jr. organized the Progressive Party, which dominated state politics for more than a decade.

It is rare these days that political heroes can rise above the public's cynicism about government and politics. And it is unlikely that Wisconsin will ever see more political heroes like Belle and Robert La Follette.

Chapter 11

Cliffhanger rescue

Dona Miller

Dona Miller was hanging clothes on a line outside her Eau Claire home on a day in late April of 1961. Her son, Chuck, was playing in the yard with a neighbor boy, Lloyd Lium, a chunky, freckle-faced lad. Both boys were eight years old.

The Millers had lived in the Third Street home for seven months, after moving from St. Cloud, Minnesota. Beyond the backyard was a steep cliff that fell away into the Chippewa River. Mrs. Miller had been concerned about the safety of that cliff since moving into the home and she hoped that the city would put up a fence.

Suddenly, she heard Chuck calling for help. She rushed over to the embankment. Chuck was pointing down into the water. He told her that Lloyd had tripped and fallen over the cliff. Mrs. Miller looked down into the water and she could see Lloyd's jacket.

She didn't hesitate, however, and started immediately down the seventy-foot embankment, sliding, falling and knowing she probably couldn't get back up. Her full skirt added to the misery and, somewhere during the ordeal, she lost her shoes. She grabbed at trees and bushes along the way to slow her descent, then slid down a vertical rock and into the forty-degree water. Mrs. Miller was a poor swimmer but she managed to swim fifteen feet over to Lloyd, through water twenty-five feet deep.

A petite woman, she wasn't much bigger than the boy. She knew the swift current could carry both of them downstream toward the open gates of a dam. She grabbed Lloyd's belt and towed him back to the base of the cliff. She put one hand on a rock and used the other to hold Lloyd's head above the water. Her nine-year-old daughter, Patty, was standing at the top of the embankment and Mrs. Miller shouted to her to run to the nearby H&H Grocery for help.

Out on the river, Gary Kruger was water-skiing. In the boat were twin brothers, Orville and Orvie Frank. As Kruger skied by her, Mrs. Miller shouted to him but he couldn't hear her over the noise of the boat's motor.

The Franks eventually turned the boat around and headed back. As they approached, Mrs. Miller shouted to Kruger again, and, this time, he heard her calls. Kruger motioned to the men in the boat, then dropped his tow rope and skis, swimming over to Mrs. Miller and the boy. Kruger helped hold up Lloyd's head while the boat circled back for them.

The boat took Lloyd and Mrs. Miller to the Riverview landing and Lloyd was rushed to Luther Hospital, where he was treated for scratches and bruises suffered in the fall. Due to the quick action of Mrs. Miller, his injuries weren't serious. Mrs. Miller refused treatment for her scratches and bruises but said she did feel better after a hot bath.

Police Sgt. Arthur Neuser, said Mrs. Miller's rescue was one of the most heroic acts he'd heard about during his 24 years on the force: "It took a lot of nerve to do what she did and most people would have thought twice before trying to get down that bank."

Three days later, the *Eau Claire Leader* also praised Mrs. Miller in an editorial: "She could have been excused if her mother love made her hug her own small son in thankfulness that he was safe. But she didn't stop there."

Mrs. Miller was awarded a bronze medal and $500 from the Carnegie Hero Fund Commission for her efforts in saving Lloyd Lium.

She and her husband, Charles, brought several neighbors to the next meeting of the City Council. They pleaded with city officials to erect a fence along the cliff, which ran behind the Third Street homes for about five blocks.

"Last year, they talked about putting up a fence," Mrs. Miller said. "Perhaps a near tragedy like this will help the city to act quickly."

Not long after the incident, the Millers moved to Rice Lake and later settled in the Minneapolis area.

Lium, who still lives in Eau Claire, said he thinks the family moved because of publicity surrounding the incident. He and his wife, Sharon, have two children.

Lium studied to become a teacher but couldn't land a teaching job. He held a job for a while in retail sales and now works as a night custodian. He said the near-drowning incident was his only close call. He also said the city did finally put up a fence on the ridge.

"It's a joke," he said. "It's just like maybe three-feet high. You can jump over it."

Chapter 12

Twice a hero
Gary Wetzel

War is an ugly business and few wars in recent times have been uglier than the war in Vietnam. Not only was support for the war shaky at home but the war was fought in a steamy jungle and the enemy often was civilians.

Gary Wetzel, of Oak Creek, Wisconsin, was among thousands of Wisconsin young men drafted to serve in Vietnam. He was among the few who would emerge heroes.

Wetzel was sent to Vietnam in October 1966. He was a young man of average build with a toothy grin and a flat-top haircut. It was a time when the war still was supported by a majority of Americans and before the nation had grown weary of the elusiveness in attaining meaningful victory.

Wetzel's first choice was the Marines but he needed

a recommendation from his high school, where he'd punched the dean of boys and been expelled. So he settled for the Army instead. Although he hadn't finished high school, he passed his high school equivalency exam at Fort Knox.

When he came home in August 1966, Wetzel noticed something had changed. Hanging out at Betty's Chocolate Shop just wasn't the same after the intense experience of combat. He got tired of drinking beer with the old gang or talking about cars. When he watched coverage of the war on TV news, he wanted to be back. He returned to Vietnam by Thanksgiving.

In January 1968, the North Vietnamese and Vietcong launched a major assault, seizing twenty-eight provincial capitals. When they were forced to retreat, they left villages and cities in flames.

Wetzel, assigned as a helicopter door gunner, was a veteran warrior who knew the dangers of battle. He hoped to become a pilot. On Jan. 8, his chopper was flying low in a dangerous area near Ap Dong An when it got hit, skidded and stopped. The aircraft commander, a friend of Wetzel's, was wounded and he scrambled from his post to drag his commander out the door to safety. A grenade exploded four feet behind the men and Wetzel fell back into the mud. He raised his gun and fired, hitting another enemy soldier who was about to throw another grenade.

As Wetzel slowly got to his feet, he realized part of his left arm had been shot off. He also had been wounded in the right arm, chest and left leg. He took the remaining portion of his arm and stuck it in his

Madison Newspapers Inc. newsroom library

Accompanied by Bonnie Kline, his fiancée, Gary Wetzel receives the Congressional Medal of Honor from Gov. Warren Knowles.

belt, then ran around to the front of the chopper, where he'd dropped the commander. Using his right hand, put tourniquets on the commander's legs. Then he dropped to the ground and played dead as enemy soldiers closed in and started killing the wounded. They came up to the chopper and tried to remove Wetzel's machine gun. Sliding on his belly, he moved around the chopper, and fired, killing eight men. When he moved back to the front of the chopper, the commander was awake.

"Tell Jane I love her," the commander said. Wetzel refused, saying he knew they both would be rescued. But the commander died moments later.

Wetzel ran for the safety of a nearby dike across a

rice field. Halfway there, he was hit in the leg, went down and passed out. Somehow, he staggered back to his gun well and opened fire on an enemy bunker. He hit an explosive charge and suddenly saw more than two dozen bodies of enemy soldiers fly into the air.

A medic was shot near the rice dike and couldn't move, so Wetzel began dragging wounded American soldiers over to him for treatment. Fighting shock and nausea, he later estimated dragging ten or fifteen wounded soldiers over to the medic.

"I figured I had enough spunk in me and I didn't want to die in a lousy rice paddy," he told author Timothy Lowry in *And Brave Men, Too.* "So I got one more guy out and just laid there."

Irv Wells, another Oak Creek native, was a member of the medical team who rescued Wetzel and his crew. Certainly they all would have been killed if not for Wetzel's courage, which never failed him despite severe wounds. "They counted 116 dead enemy troops from his particular gun," Wells said.

Wetzel was sent home and, in December, he was awarded the Congressional Medal of Honor by Wisconsin Gov. Warren Knowles. He was the third Wisconsin man to receive the honor during the Vietnam War and the 38th ever in the state. When he got home, Wetzel called his commander's girlfriend to tell her the man's dying words.

After the war, Wetzel got a job at Ladish Forge in Cudahy. Like quite a few Vietnam veterans, he had some difficulty adjusting to civilian life. He studied welding engineering for a while in junior college. He said he'd miss at least one shift a week because he was drunk and, finally, after a year he was fired. He also worked construction jobs.

Wetzel and his wife, Bonnie, had two children but, to him, nothing in civilian life seemed to match the thrill of combat.

"Once it's over and you get time to think about it, you can't top it," he told Timothy Lowry. "Nothing can top that high."

But Wetzel's discharge wasn't the end of his heroism.

In April 1977, he spotted a car on fire on a South Milwaukee street as he and his wife were driving home. Wetzel rushed to the burning car and used his right arm to pull Edward Miller from the wreckage.

"If the gas tank would have gone, we both would have been goners," Wetzel said afterward.

In the early 1970s, he headed north to Alaska to work on the Alaskan oil pipeline. By 1982, he was unemployed, a condition he called "between successes."

Without a job, Wetzel launched a fund drive to raise money for renting buses to take veterans to Washington, D.C. that year for the dedication of the Vietnam Veterans Memorial. He took out a personal loan for $1,800 after the fund drive failed to muster enough money.

But when Wetzel's generosity became known, "nickels and dimes came pouring in," he said. More than enough money was collected but Wetzel refused to keep any of the excess for his trouble.

"We have $127 left over, enough to buy turkey

and all the trimmings for some needy Vietnam veterans for Thanksgiving," he said.

Wetzel describes his Vietnam experience in a four-minute video shown at the Wisconsin War Museum in Madison. He wears his medal proudly around his neck. He's older now, not the brash young kid who served his country so well He describes his courageous act in a matter-of-fact style and with a distinct humility.

It is not often someone gets two opportunities to show their courage in one lifetime. Gary Wetzel not only got two chances but also had an opportunity to show his dedication to his fellow veterans in peace as well as war.

Chapter 13

Championship coach
Dianne Holum

D ianne Holum achieved worldwide renown before she attended the University of Wisconsin-Madison at age 20. A native of Northbrook, Illinois, Holum won two speed-skating medals in the 1972 Winter Olympics.

When she came to Madison later that year, she decided to put skating behind her and concentrate on her studies. She majored in physical education with a minor in Scandinavian studies.

"I really didn't intend to get this involved in it," she said. "But the kids have been so great. They're so determined. We've had fantastic workouts."

Fortunately, she couldn't put skating behind her, for Holum's heroic status is due more to her coaching than to her own skating career. Over the next decade, Holum would be responsible for several Wisconsinbred Olympic medalists, including Beth and Eric Heiden and Sarah and Mary Docter.

Holum was the only double-medal winner for the United States in the 1968 winter games at Grenoble, France. As a 16-year-old, she won silver and bronze medals. Between 1968 and 1972, she trained in the Netherlands. At that time, Dutch skaters had a lock on most of the speed-skating medals but it was a domination that Holum was determined to break.

In 1972 at Sapporo, Japan, she won a gold medal in the 1,500-meter race with an Olympic record speed of 2 minutes, 20.85 seconds. In the 3,000-meter race, she finished second to a Dutch skater. Her teammate from her hometown of Northbrook, Anne Henning, won gold and silver medals in two races.

The year of 1972 was a tumultuous one for college students across the nation. American soldiers were dying in Vietnam. The memory of the Kent State University shootings lingered in the minds of many. George McGovern was making his bid for President on an anti-war platform and many students volunteered in his campaign.

Holum was named chairwoman of the University of Wisconsin-Madison Nixonettes, part of a national network of young people supporting the re-election of President Richard Nixon. More significant than her political activity, however, was the fact that Holum helped organize four indoor skating meets at the Hartmeyer Arena in Madison. It was here that her brilliant coaching career began.

She brought to Madison an emphasis on a metric

skating style that became popular in the Winter Olympics. She also brought to Madison the Northbrook style of self-discipline that made that city the skating capital of the world for a short time in the early 1970s. Holum's philosophy was that speed skating success is due more to hard work than raw athletic ability.

And so, during the summer, the Heidens and the Docters often frequented the Odana Hills Golf Course but not to enjoy a lazy afternoon on the links. In ninety-degree heat, they would jog along a fairway, then stop under a tree for vigorous skating exercises and dry skating maneuvers on the grass instead of ice. The workouts lasted two hours and the young skaters would come back for more in the evening. Holum's skill was at grooming young skaters, beginning at age 13 or 14. Unlike the European practice at the time, she coached men as well as women.

"That's the American way," she said. "They're much more chauvinistic in Europe. In Sweden or Norway, the girls wouldn't think of training with boys. Europeans can't comprehend me coaching the men. It would be like a girl coaching a pro football team here."

Today, male coaches of women skaters are common. But not every Olympic skater wanted to train with Holum. At the 1976 Winter Olympics, Holum and Peter Schotting shared coaching duties for the Olympic skaters. Dan Immerfall, another Olympic star from Madison, trained with Schotting.

Holum's Republican political bent came through again in a 1979 interview in the *Wisconsin State Journal,* where she said she preferred private to government sponsors.

"It takes the government so long to make any decisions," she said. "I really would hate to see the government controlling athletics. It scares me."

By 1980, Holum had moved her pupils to the Petit Ice Arena in West Allis. The Olympic-sized ice arena had been built in 1966 for $585,720. At the Winter Olympics that year, the benefits of her rigorous training would pay off. Eric Heiden won five gold medals and the U.S. team won a total of eight. Perhaps figuring she was unlikely to top that performance, Holum resigned as coach of the U.S. Olympic team. She was replaced by Bob Corby of Madison and Peter Mueller, a retired Olympic skater.

"I really don't know where I'm going to go," she said. "I would like to go out West but it's a matter of jobs. I'm just going to take a nice long break. In skating you have to be so dedicated and it never allows you much time for anything else."

Holum did go West to Colorado, where she was hired to work with the Colorado Rockies, then considered the worst team in the National Hockey League. She put the hockey players through her rigorous dry skating maneuvers.

"With a good dry-land program, you get on the ice and feel like you've never been off it," she said.

Despite her decision to retire, Holum said she gained more satisfaction from coaching than from winning her own medals: "As an athlete, you are only concerned with yourself. Coaching is more rewarding."

But Holum's retirement was temporary. Squabbles with the U.S. International Skating Association caused both Corby and Mueller to resign in 1983 and Holum was back at the helm. She didn't mince words at what she viewed as the problem with Corby and Mueller,

Madison Newspapers Inc. newsroom library
Dianne Holum

blaming Corby for undermining the team's confidence:

"Bob has a big interest in working with elite, and mainly with elite men," she said. "If Bob was doing such a fantastic job, 35 skaters wouldn't have left him and voted for someone else as coach. I've had a heck of a time this year trying to get the skaters I'm working with to believe in things, to have confidence, because they lost a lot of that the last few years."

Despite the rift between them, Holum and Corby continued to prepare their charges for the 1984 games at Sarajevo, Yugoslavia. Among Corby's pupils was an 18-year-old named Dan Jansen of Milwaukee, later to star in the 1994 Winter Olympics.

Holum also worried about the future of skating, a sport that doesn't generate college scholarships or the attention of hockey. "This sport can crumble ten years from now, when our clubs fall apart," she said. "And they're going to fall apart unless they can interest a lot more young people."

By the early 1990s, Jansen and Milwaukee speed-skating star Bonnie Blair were carrying on the tradition of skating excellence that Holum brought to Wisconsin in 1972. In 1994, Holum was among the first women elected to the Wisconsin Sports Hall of Fame. And she had a new Olympic hopeful under her wing, putting the young woman through the regimen of dry skating and hard work. The pupil was her daughter, Kirsten.

Chapter 14

Red Cloud's last stand

Mitchell Red Cloud

Corporal Mitchell Red Cloud stood guard as his Company E of the 19th Infantry was bedded down near Chonghyon, Korea.

Standing guard that night of November 4, 1950, meant Red Cloud occupied the last foxhole. It would be his task to keep watch and warn other soldiers scattered in holes and ditches along a ridge of an attack.

A month earlier, the balance in the Korean War had shifted dramatically when over 100,000 Chinese Communist troops slipped across the Yalu River to confront United Nations forces.

For the first time in American history, a clear-cut victory would not be won in this war. It was a situation that would be repeated more than a decade later in Vietnam.

"But as is often seems of unpleasant national experiences, the Korean War is one of those events which most Americans, once it ended, were eager to permit to slip through the crevices of memory," author Joseph C. Goulden writes in *Korea: The Untold Story of the War.*

All was well after United Nations forces came on the scene the previous summer and swept back North Korean troops. The true nemesis was the Soviet Union and part of America's agenda in entering the war was to battle the Soviets.

Chinese and Soviet leaders met that fall and, although the Soviets decided not to get directly involved, they gave approval for the Chinese to enter the war. The Chinese presence wasn't felt at first. By early November, however, they had brought about a dramatic shift in the fortunes of United Nations forces.

The Chinese troops often used the strategy of attacking from the rear, cutting off supply lines and routes of retreat, before making a frontal assault. Many American soldiers were slain while they slept in their sleeping bags. In one attack, 105-millimeter howitzers were turned on the advancing Chinese troops at point-blank range. In another attack, Australian troops beat back the Chinese with bayonets.

The close, personal nature of this war was in sharp contrast to the end of World War II, when nuclear weapons persuaded the Japanese to surrender.

So it was this cool November night as Red Cloud, a Native American from Friendship, Wisconsin, kept his eyes and ears open for movement beyond his foxhole. When a surge of Chinese troops was less than a hundred feet from his foxhole, Red Cloud spotted them. He rose halfway out of the hole and shouted to the other soldiers, then began firing with his automatic weapon.

Red Cloud fired and watched a few enemy soldiers crumple to the ground but still they came — soldier after soldier. As they returned fire, a burst from an enemy weapon knocked Red Cloud to the ground. He stood up, wrapping his arm around a tree limb to steady himself, and resumed firing again and again at rush of enemy soldiers.

At age 26, Red Cloud was no raw recruit. His mother lived in a converted automobile trailer and he had grown up in poverty. The military offered an opportunity and he grabbed it before the Japanese attack on Pearl Harbor. Although he wasn't yet 18, Red Cloud had dropped out of high school to join the Marines, where he won an expert rifleman's badge. Away from his mother's home cooking, he lost eighty pounds from his induction until his discharge three years later.

Red Cloud served his country on Midway Island and during the worst fighting at Guadalcanal. He also was a member of Carlson's Raiders, an elite fighting unit of the South Pacific.

When the Korean War began, he enlisted this time in the Army. Now, he was in the thick of the fighting, protecting his company from wave after wave of Chinese Communist soldiers. He kept firing, watching a couple of enemy soldiers go down, but ultimately the numbers were against him. Mitchell Red Cloud was shot and died.

His heroic act, however, in holding off hundreds of enemy soldiers gave his company just enough time to gather up the wounded and retreat to safety. When the dust cleared and American troops returned to the battlefield, they saw many enemy soldiers who had died from Red Cloud's gun.

The following spring, his mother, Nellie Red Cloud, left her trailer for a trip to Washington, D.C., where she accepted the posthumous award of the Congressional Medal of Honor on behalf of her son, who had given his life, not only for his comrades, but for his country.

Chapter 15

Cancer warrior
Howard Martin Temin

H oward Temin was a soldier in a battle far more chronic and deadly than Vietnam, Korea or World War II. Temin was one of the world's leading genetic researchers who worked diligently to find a cure for cancer and, later, studied the HIV virus, widely accepted as the cause of AIDS.

But Temin, who won the Nobel Prize for his cancer research, wasn't satisfied to hide away in his lab at the University of Wisconsin's McArdle Laboratory for Cancer Research.

He was born on Dec. 10, 1934, in Philadelphia and, even as a teen-ager, he had a consuming interest in science. He published his first scientific paper at age 18, then went to Swarthmore College, graduating in 1955. He did graduate work at California Institute of Technology in Pasadena, studying under Renato

Madison Newspapers Inc. newsroom library

Howard Temin

Dulbecco, a pioneer of modern biology. After receiving his doctorate at Cal Tech in 1959, Temin came to the University of Wisconsin.

During the 1950s, Temin began studying chicken retroviruses — not considered a promising endeavor at the time. Through his research, Temin developed a theory that RNA (ribonucleic acid) could enter a cell and change the DNA (deoxyribonucleic acid). Before that time, scientists believed genetic information flowed only in one direction — from DNA to RNA.

Working with Satoshi Mizutani, a post-doctoral student, Temin's carried out important research, advancing the theory that viruses can cause cancer. In 1975, he and two other cancer researchers were awarded the Nobel Prize. Sharing the prize were Temin's mentor, Dulbecco, and David Baltimore of the Massachusetts Institute of Technology. Baltimore had proven a theory similar to Temin's.

Besides the Nobel Prize, Temin was the recipient of an $843,000 grant from the American Cancer Society to offset his university salary. He was featured in a 1971 Newsweek cover story on cancer research. He was elected to the National Academy of Sciences and received awards for his research from the Bertner Foundation, the Gairdner Foundation and the Albert Lasker medical research award. In 1982, he was named a Steenbock Professor of Biological Science. In 1987, he was appointed by President Reagan to the National Cancer Institute Advisory Board. He won the National Medal of Science in 1992.

Temin's work not only opened the door to the

modern age of cancer research but his discovery of reverse transcriptase led scientists to find and identify the HIV virus. His research appeared to indicate that viruses can cause cancer, but Temin said environmental causes of cancer were easier to control.

"This kind of research indicated probably much of human cancer is caused by environmental carcinogens (cancer-causing agents) and it's easier to decrease cancer by decreasing them," he said.

The nation's leading carcinogen comes from the smoking of cigarettes and Temin used his influence to combat smoking. When Temin went to Stockholm to accept his Nobel Prize, he lost no time in launching his anti-smoking crusade. He bowed to King Carl Gustaf and turned to the audience, complaining that people were smoking while he was being honored for his cancer research.

"I am outraged at the lack of measures taken to stop smoking," he said. "To achieve a decrease in cigarette smoking is the most important goal today."

He testified before a U.S. Senate committee, urging the senators to hike the federal cigarette tax from eight cents per pack in 1976 to as high as fifty cents per pack. He told a group of insurance company executives they should begin charging higher rates for smokers and heavy drinkers. He suggested that the federal government pay tobacco farmers to stop growing it. In 1979, Temin was excused from serving on the jury in the Barbara Hoffman murder trial after he complained of smoking by fellow jurors. Hoffman, accused of killing a Stoughton, Wisconsin man, was one of Madison's most notorious murderers of the era.

Temin could have used his worldwide status to build a larger lab or enhance his own prestige. But the humble researcher with a shock of unruly dark hair continued life as usual, riding his bicycle to work at his small lab. In 1981, he wrote a guest column for the *Wisconsin State Journal* against violence. Just months after the hostage crisis in Iran, Temin wrote that the nation's emphasis on military force may encourage domestic violence.

"I believe a person in my position may have a special responsibility to speak out about the rising tide of violence that threatens the health (security) of our societies and people," he wrote.

Temin said it may be appropriate for a cancer researcher to comment on violence because "cancer is a kind of violence, a disease where a part of the body wars on the rest."

Temin was the third Nobel Prize winner at the University of Wisconsin. The others were Har Gobind Khorana, winner of a 1968 Nobel Prize for his study of nucleic acid chemistry, and Joshua Lederberg, who won a 1958 Nobel Prize for his studies on the organization of genetic material in bacteria.

After a year of his own personal struggle with cancer, Temin died at age 59, somewhat ironically of adenocarcinoma, a form of lung cancer not associated with smoking. At the time of Temin's death, his anti-smoking crusade finally was beginning to bear fruit in Wisconsin and around the nation.

Chapter 16

A boy and a train
Harold Birkholz

Young David Knutson was playing with his brother and sister in the yard of their Brodhead home on April 26, 1963. When Dawn Ann, 6, and Douglas, 4, went into the house, David, 2, stayed outside. As two-year-old children will do, he wandered away.

An hour later, David's mother called the police to report him missing. His father was summoned from his job in Rockton as officers began a house-to-house search for the boy.

Harold Birkholz was the fireman on a freight train headed from Janesville to Mineral Point. Eugene Peterson was the engineer. As the train passed through Brodhead, about one-and-a-half miles from the Knutson home, Peterson thought he spotted something on the trestle up ahead. David somehow had wandered on to the trestle and sat down between the tracks with his back to the approaching train.

Although the train was moving at 25 miles per hour and Peterson immediately applied the brakes, Birkholz knew it was hopeless — that the huge diesel locomotive couldn't possibly stop in time.

The engine jerked and Birkholz left the cab, moving to the side steps. He went down them backwards and stepped on to a foot board at the front of the engine. He grabbed a rail, then crouched and extended his arm. The engine, still jerking wildly as Peterson desperately tried to slow it down, was less than two feet from the boy and still moving at eight miles per hour. Birkholz knew he would get just one chance to save the boy. If he failed, the child would be crushed beneath the slow-moving train.

Birkholz grabbed the back of David's shirt and lifted him quickly but his feet went under the foot board. The veteran trainman stood up but, as he pulled the boy, the shirt began to tear. Birkholz held David tightly against his chest as the train traveled ninety feet farther and stopped.

Birkholz and David scrambled into the cab. Peterson put the locomotive into reverse and headed back to a station. At this point, the trainmen had no idea who the boy was because he couldn't tell them his name.

David was rushed to the Stuessy Clinic for treatment of scratches he received from crawling under a barbed-wire fence. On the clinic examining table, he cried, "Mamma." It was one of few words he could speak. At 12:30 p.m., David's parents were told that he was safe.

After his ordeal, David was hungry. When he got home, he ate two bowls of soup, crackers, milk and a piece of cake.

Birkholz was awarded a bronze medal and $750 from the Carnegie Hero Fund Commission for his bravery in rescuing David Knutson from certain death.

Knutson still lives in Brodhead with his wife, Karen, and their two children. He works as a machinist in Beloit.

Although he has no memory of the incident, he thinks about it from time to time. He met Birkholz again several years after the incident. Fortunately, Knutson said, the train has been his only close call.

Chapter 17

An eagle leads the charge
Old Abe

Wisconsin's most famous war hero isn't a man. He's an eagle named Old Abe, who inspired troops from an Eau Claire regiment during the Civil War.

The feats of Old Abe are legendary. It was said that the eagle fought alongside Union soldiers, dive-bombing, scratching and biting Confederate troops. It was said that Old Abe frequently conducted reconnaissance missions, diving in and stealing battle plans right out of the handles of southern generals.

These extraordinary accomplishments probably didn't happen quite like that. But it's clear that Old Abe provided a lot of inspiration and entertainment during a war aggravated by widespread disease among the troops.

Old Abe seemed almost human due to his habit of

spreading his wings and screeching whenever he heard applause or cheers. He also was raised in captivity, which made him more amenable to domestication. He participated in 37 battles and, after the war, found a career as a political fund-raiser and entertainer.

In 1861, Margaret McCann of Jim Falls traded a bushel of corn with to a band of Chippewa Indians for a young eaglet that was to become Old Abe. An Indian leader known as Charley or Chief Sky (Ogemawegezhig) had shot Old Abe's mother, leaving the young eagle without food.

Old Abe's brother or sister died but the young eagle survived under Margaret McCann's care. She tied a blue ribbon around his neck and fashioned a cage from an old barrel. His wings were clipped and his foot tethered to prevent escape. The McCann children supplied the growing eagle with tasty meals of rabbits, mice and partidges.

Besides not having to work for a regular diet, Old Abe also developed an affection for music. When Margaret's husband, Dan, played the fiddle, the bird often hopped up and down and fluttered his wings.

When Dan McCann heard of a company of Civil War volunteers forming in Chippewa Falls, he offered Old Abe as a mascot. The company rejected the eagle but a similar company in Eau Claire took him under their wing after a tavern owner donated $2.50 to buy him from McCann.

Along with his regiment, Old Abe's first assignment was to basic training at Camp Randall in Madison. The eagle assumed a regular spot to the left of the flags as part of the regiment's color guard. Curiosity seekers ranging from young children to the governor flocked to Camp Randall to get a look at the young eagle.

In October 1861, Old Abe's regiment began its journey south to join the battle. As the company marched through St. Louis, southern advocates taunted the eagle, calling him a crow and a goose. Old Abe apparently became so agitated at the cries that he escaped, leading the regiment on a chase through various streets and alleys. He finally landed on a sidewalk and was recaptured by a police officer.

When the regiment was stationed at Cairo, Illinois for several months, Old Abe befriended a dog named Frank. The two animals shared rabbits and other food. They also entertained the troops with their antics. Dogs and Old Abe got along well, but he didn't like mules or steamships.

At Fredericktown, Missouri, Old Abe's Eighth Wisconsin regiment prepared for its first battle. But after coming within a mile of Confederate troops, the regiment was sent away from the lines when an accidental musket discharge killed one of the men. Before the regiment would fight its first full-scale battle, over a hundred men would die in a measles epidemic.

In fact, it wasn't until May 1862 at Farmington, Mississippi that the regiment got involved in combat. Among those mortally wounded was Capt. John Perkins, who had named Old Abe back in Eau Claire. Before he was wounded, Perkins ordered the eagle's keeper, James McGinnes, to move the animal to safety.

State Historical Society of Wisconsin

Old Abe

Old Abe imitated the soldiers. When they lay down to take cover from shelling, the eagle swooped down to the ground. When they got up, he returned to his perch, flapping his wings.

The next major battle for Old Abe and his regiment was at Corinth, Mississippi in the fall of 1862. Bullets hit his leash, breaking it, and the eagle took off, flying up and down the Union lines. He lost several wing and tail feathers in the gunfire. The flight fed the myth of Old Abe's reconnaissance missions but his wings were cropped to prevent it from happening again.

During long periods of inactivity, Old Abe often provided the entertainment. He would steal clothes from a line or food roasting over an unattended fire. He also was known to get into stashes of alcohol, suffering its effects after he drank too much.

After joining the Vicksburg, Mississippi campaign during the spring of 1863, the Eighth Regiment participated with General Sherman in the march of Union troops across Mississippi and Louisiana. After a long siege in 1864 along the Red River to capture Shreveport, Louisiana, many members of the regiment were granted a furlough. Old Abe accompanied the men back to Eau Claire.

But the eagle's furlough wasn't destined to be one of rest and relaxation. He participated in Fourth of July activities at Chippewa Falls. Shortly afterward, the eagle was headed south again with the Eighth Regiment to rejoin the battle. Old Abe and his companions were thrown into battle, clashing with Confederate troops in Missouri, Arkansas and, finally, at Nashville, Tennessee.

By the time the war ended, Old Abe was a national hero. When he returned to Wisconsin, the eagle was classified as a war relic belonging to the state. He was given a two-room apartment in the basement of the state Capitol and often could be seen enjoying himself on the Capitol Square. During one of several escapes from his keeper, the eagle attacked a flock of doves.

But Old Abe didn't spend all of his time at home because his fame made him much in demand. From Boston to Milwaukee, he was the star attraction at a series of fairs held to raise money for soldier hospitals. At a Chicago fair, his presence helped raise nearly $300,000. Thousands of photographs and lithographs of the eagle were sold.

When war hero Lucius Fairchild was elected Wisconsin governor in 1866, Old Abe became a stalwart of his administration. Fairchild tailored his campaign to appeal to veterans and Old Abe was a fixture in his efforts to organize them. The eagle often appeared at speeches, wildly flapping his wings and screeching when the music played.

Old Abe's glory years ended, however, in 1872, when C.C. Washburn was elected governor and the eagle's political mentor, Fairchild, accepted a diplomatic appointment in Russia. Not only was Old Abe's care neglected but he was forced to share his quarters with a golden eagle named Andy Johnson, who had been the Civil War mascot of another regiment. A fierce rivalry developed until Old Abe murdered Andy Johnson in early 1874. After appearing at two rain-soaked rallies the following year, the eagle suffered health problems. His personality also appeared to change as he became more cantankerous toward his human friends.

In 1876, he played a major role in the nation's centennial celebration. His appearances in Washington, D.C. brought the eagle to prominence once again and requests were received for him to appear throughout the nation. When he was home in the state Capitol, a steady stream of visitors came to see the famous Wisconsin eagle. Among them was young Jane Addams, who later would play a major role in developing neighborhood houses social service programs. She is best known for founding Hull House.

In February 1881, a small fire in the basement of the Capitol sent heavy black smoke billowing through the eagle's quarters. Afterward, Old Abe refused to eat. He went into spasms a month later and died March 25 in his keeper's arms.

Veterans volunteered to serve as Old Abe's pall-bearers but it was decided he should be preserved through taxidermy and mounted in the Capitol. A glass case was installed to enclose the eagle's body. The stuffed bird continued to travel, making appearances at veterans' events far and wide. He was moved to a place of honor at the State Historical Society. Just as Elvis myths would abound a century later after the death of that legendary entertainer, Old Abe's death only fueled the outlandish tales about his exploits in battle.

The most curious issue, however, arose in 1889, when a *Milwaukee Sentinel* article asserted that Old Abe actually was female because he once laid an egg. That issue never was resolved definitively.

In April 1903, Old Abe's remains were moved back to the state Capitol in the G.A.R. Memorial Hall. It was to be a fateful move, however, for the eagle suffered a second death. In early 1904, fire destroyed the Capitol and, with it, the stuffed eagle.

As in the case of Elvis, the loss of the original eagle prompted a plethora of copies, both in statues and replicas. From Vicksburg to Camp Randall, monuments were erected to Old Abe.

The original feathers and beak may be long gone but the spirit of Old Abe remains even today. A long-time mascot of the state Assembly, a replica of Old Abe was moved to temporary chambers in 1994 when the Assembly was forced to vacate the Capitol for remodeling. Old Abe had become the most dramatic symbol of the Assembly chamber.

Chapter 18

Ice rescue

Jennifer Beyer

On Valentine's Day in Appleton, anyone might expect that the ice on the Fox River would be thick enough to walk on. At least that's what nine-year-old Colin Deeg and a friend thought that afternoon in 1992 when they tried to cross a navigational canal of the river. But the boys didn't know the ice was paper-thin and, when they got part of the way to the other side, it cracked open, plunging Colin into frigid water six feet deep. Colin's friend tried to pull him out and, when that failed, he scrambled for help.

The family of Jennifer Beyer, age 22, had moved from Appleton to New Berlin after her high school graduation four years earlier. She was working as a nanny, taking care of young children in Northbrook, Illinois. On this Valentine's Day, she had returned to visit her hometown of Appleton. As she was driving by the canal about 5:30 p.m., she spotted a boy waving frantically for her to stop.

"It took me a minute to realize he was all wet," Beyer later told the *Appleton Post Crescent.* "The look on his face — I pulled over and went from there."

While Jennifer headed for the canal, the boy ran to TLC Gift Baskets, a store in the Between the Locks shopping mall. He explained what was wrong to Cyndy Graf and Kenton Keeton and the pair headed for the canal.

They watched Jennifer as she started across the ice, trying to reach Colin, who was about forty-five feet from the bank. When she heard the ice crack, Jennifer got down on her hands and knees to crawl the rest of the way. As she crept closer to the boy, she tried to pass her scarf to Colin, hoping he could grab it and she could pull him out. Suddenly, the ice broke again and Jennifer fell through into the ice-cold water.

With her body partially submerged, Jennifer moved closer to Colin. She tried to pull him out of the water but couldn't lift the boy. She tried to break the ice toward the shore, hoping she could break off enough to reach the shore through the water or, at least, to find solid ice. When that didn't work, she grabbed his head and held it above the water so he wouldn't go under. With her other hand, she clutched the edge of the ice. Colin passed out and, as her body grew numb in the cold water, Jennifer had trouble staying awake herself.

"All I could do was hold on to the ice with one hand and the boy with the other," she said. "I was sure it was all over."

As Graf and Keeton reached the canal, they heard Jennifer screaming.

"I can't breathe!" she shouted, still submerged in the freezing water.

"I'm coming!" Graf shouted back. "Hang in there!"

Cyndy and Kenton tried to crawl out on the ice but it kept breaking under them. Finally, Graf got close enough to Colin to grab his hair and hold his head out of the water.

"I've never been on frozen water, on a frozen lake or anything," she said. "You just think, 'There is a kid.' Afterward, I thought, 'My God, I was on the ice.'"

Cyndy had rushed out of the shop so quickly that she lost an estimated $900 in receipts and her car keys. She helped hold Jennifer from going under until several police officers arrived and pulled them out. When he was pulled out of the water, Colin's body temperature was 79 degrees and some people thought he wouldn't survive.

"When they carried him off the ice, I could see the heart monitor and it was going," Kenton said. "The line was going up and down."

Colin was taken to Children's Hospital of Wauwatosa, where he drifted in and out of consciousness. Paramedics and doctors, using a blood bypass machine to warm his body, were able to revive Colin. His blood was pumped out, warmed up and then pumped back into his body. He was treated for hypothermia and hospitalized for a week. Jennifer also was treated for hypothermia, and both recovered.

The actions of Jennifer, Cyndy and Kenton in try-ing to rescue Colin are a contrast to the residents of a nearby house where Colin's friend first sought help but was turned away.

"I think that is the saddest thing," Kenton said. "That makes me want to cry. The boy was completely drenched."

The following year, Jennifer Beyer was awarded a hero medal and a $2,500 grant from the Carnegie Hero Fund Commission for her daring attempt to rescue Colin Deeg. Although Jennifer had remained calm and cool-headed while saving Colin, the an-nouncement of the award caused a less controlled re-action.

"I screamed," she said. "At least half of the money will go right in the bank. It will help out next year."

"That's just great," Colin's father, Randy, said of the award. "I always thought she deserved it. We all thought she earned it. Jennifer," the father said, "is definitely a hero. He saved our boy's life."

Chapter 19

Shooting to wound

Louis Molnar

P olice officers often are heroes in small ways, providing needed help to someone at just the right moment. The job always carries a risk and some police officers become heroes when they lose their lives in the line of duty. But police officers certainly aren't supernatural, however, and a heroic deed can carry a psychological price. Such was the case with Lou Molnar, a Dane County sheriff's deputy.

Just past noon on January 15, 1988, young Aaron Lindh was angry when he went to Madison's City-County Building to pay a ticket. He went into a stairwell and walked up and down several times but the physical exertion failed to dissipate the anger he felt. Lindh left the building and returned with a rifle.

He walked down a basement hallway to the sheriff's office, where two people were standing at the counter.

Lindh aimed the rifle and fired, then watched a man and woman crumple to the floor in a pool of blood. Eleanor Townsend, a secretary in the corporation counsel's office, was killed. Erik Erickson, a state employee, would recover from his wounds.

Lindh left the sheriff's office and continued down the basement hallway until he got to the end and walked in the county coroner's office. Spotting the rifle, at least one employee dived under her desk. But Coroner Clyde Chamberlain tried a different approach. Chamberlain tried to reason with Lindh, asking him to put the rifle down so no one would get hurt. Lindh responded by lifting the barrel and firing again, killing Chamberlain.

In their nearby evidence lab, Molnar and his boss, Lt. John Van Dinter, heard the shots and screams. They ran into the hallway just in time to see Lindh leaving the coroner's office. The two deputies drew their guns. Lindh aimed his rifle at them.

About 10 yards beyond the gunman, people were crowded into a hallway coffee shop for lunch. Molnar and Van Dinter knew that if Lindh turned toward the coffee shop, more people likely would be killed or wounded.

"I'm going to kill everybody," Lindh told the deputies. "I'm going to kill you."

Molnar shouted down the hallway, advising the people in the coffee shop to take cover. The gunman began walking toward the deputies.

"Kill me," Lindh said. "Go ahead, kill me."

Molnar aimed his revolver at the gunman's chest.

Madison Newspapers Inc. newsroom library

Louis Molnar

No one would blame him if he blew away this crazed killer right now. But something made him lower his aim to Lindh's stomach. He fired and Lindh went down.

It is difficult to estimate how many more people would have been killed that day if Molnar hadn't shot Lindh. It also would have been easy for Molnar to kill the gunman and the community probably would have applauded the move.

But Molnar showed compassion and, as he had been trained, used just enough force to stop the gunman. Lindh was convicted of two murders and the wounding of Erickson. He is serving a sentence of life plus thirty-five-and-a-half years at Columbia Correctional Institution in Portage.

Molnar didn't fit the image of a hero. Short and squat with glasses and a mustache, he was well-liked by other deputies but without the charisma and arrogance of an action-movie star. He clearly was a hero but didn't feel that way. He began drinking heavily. He grew suicidal. He was forced to deal with crank telephone callers who asked him why he didn't "blow the nigger away" or fellow deputies who asked why he didn't "finish the job" by killing Lindh.

"I was a real bastard at work," Molnar later told *Wisconsin State Journal* columnist George Hesselberg. "I didn't sleep. I didn't eat. I drank."

Molnar went on disability leave the following year and never returned to active duty with the department. He was arrested for drunken driving. He could no longer pick up a gun. Despite his heroic deed, his department and his supervisors weren't very sympathetic. The county risk manager told Molnar his emotional problems weren't work-related.

In addition, Molnar suffered nightmares. In his dreams, Molnar sometimes would empty his gun, blasting away the young gunman. Van Dinter, who didn't fire, also had his own nightmares. In Van Dinter's dreams, he would shoot at Lindh but hit a bystander behind him. The bystander would fall to the floor and Lindh would laugh.

Van Dinter was promoted to captain. Molnar was diagnosed with post-traumatic stress syndrome, the same illness that sometimes afflicts soldiers in combat.

For a while, he fought treatment but ultimately accepted it. After a long struggle with the county bureaucracy, Molnar finally retired on disability.

In a letter to the *Wisconsin State Journal,* attorney Robert Burke, who defended Lindh, praised Molnar. "Lou could have killed Aaron but made the conscious decision not to," Burke wrote. "I believe Lou could see that he was dealing with a very disturbed young man who was asking him to end his misery.

"Molnar put his life on the line and was concerned about the safety of the others in the area. I find it hard to believe that anyone would criticize his decision not to kill Aaron. He had every right of an officer to shoot to kill. His decision to wound and not to kill was a courageous act because he could see that he was dealing with a kid on a suicide mission."

During his struggles, Molnar said he wished he had been off duty that day and never got involved in the incident. But the citizens of Wisconsin and especially the people in the coffee shop are lucky this hero was on the scene.

Chapter 20

Machete attack

Russell Cera
Gary Lamberty

While they're on duty, police officers are expected to take charge of dangerous situations and play the hero once in a while. For many officers, however, this responsibility carries into their off-duty time as well.

Russell Cera, a Racine police officer, was off-duty on June 3, 1991, when he was called upon to resolve just such a dangerous situation. He wasn't carrying a gun.

Cera, who had joined the force just six months earlier, was leaving a barber shop about 4:40 p.m. when he saw a car stopped at a light at Washington and Hayes avenues. A woman, Susan Lawrence, age 38, and her two children, Cathryn and Courtney, ages 7 and 4, stepped off the curb to cross the street. Although the light was red, the driver of a pickup truck gunned his engine, moved forward and hit the women and children, seemingly on purpose.

Passersby quickly came to the aid of Lawrence and the children, who were taken to St. Mary's Hospital in Racine. Cera jumped in his car and pursued the driver. After a chase of several blocks, the pickup driver slammed into another truck stopped at a light at Washington and Lathrop avenues, causing a chain-reaction accident involving six drivers.

As soon as his truck stopped, the driver jumped out, brandishing a large two-foot-long machete with a two-inch blade. Waving the machete over his head, the crazed driver first attacked 80-year-old Stanley Hansen, cutting him on the neck and back of the head. The driver lunged at Patricia Budy, age 23, of Milwaukee, who had stopped to help anyone injured in the accident.

"Bizarre was the word for it," one witness told the *Racine Journal-Times.* "It was something out of a nightmare."

Then, the machete man smashed the window in a car driven by Sandra Vollnar, age 39, and began slashing at the woman as she sat in her car.

"He beat the hell out of her window and started slashing at her," the unidentified witness said.

If Cera were armed, he undoubtedly would have been able to stop the crazed man. A delivery truck driver tried to pin the machete man against Vollnar's car but pulled back when he saw the man could continue to attack Vollnar even if he were pinned.

Firefighters came out of a nearby stations, brandishing axes and pole hooks in an effort to restrain the crazed attacker. Cera began throwing rocks at him to distract the man from attacking other drivers. The machete man slashed at Cera, then grabbed one of the poles and hit him. Cera continued to taunt the assailant as if he were a raging bull, trying to disorient him.

Gary Lamberty, 41, a high-school math teacher, watched the melee from his nearby apartment. He picked up a branch and confronted the man, maneuvering himself between the attacker and one of his downed victims. The machete man swung hard at Lamberty, knocking the branch from his hands.

Lamberty looked around from another weapon, then saw that the man had turned his back. Seizing the moment, Lamberty charged and tackled the machete, bringing him to the ground. Cera and other men quickly joined Lamberty in subduing the man.

Lamberty had changed jobs shortly before the incident, transferring from the Brown Alternative Center to McKinley Middle School. At the alternative center, he taught Racine's most aggressive and violent youngsters.

"This was just another day at work for me," he said.

The assailant was identified as Albert Price, 35, who had a long criminal record. In 1985, Price had abducted a woman and pushed her into the path of a moving car. He also had felony convictions for armed robbery in Nashville, Tennessee and burglary in Green Bay. Price was sentenced to 185 years in prison for the machete attack and will be 82 years old before he is eligible for parole.

Cera and Lamberty received medals and reward money from the Carnegie Hero Fund Commission for their roles in subduing the vicious Price and his machete that day.

Cera still works as an officer for the Racine Police Department. Lamberty still teaches at the middle school. Both men are frequently reminded of the incident. A story appeared in 1994 in the national Globe newspaper and Lamberty appeared on the Gordon Elliott talk show.

Lamberty said he got "choked up" last winter when Cathryn Lawrence, Susan Lawrence's oldest daughter, read him a report she had written for school, praising him as her personal hero.

"To me, it wasn't such a big deal," Lamberty said. "I think there are thousands of these incidents."

Unfortunately, there aren't thousands of heroes like Cera and Lamberty.

Chapter 21

Tunnel of terror

Harris Giddings
Lawrence Hanlon
Peter Lancaster

In some cities, firefighters work flexible schedules that allow them to have second careers. A typical schedule, for example, might call for 24 hours on duty, 24 hours off and then 48 hours off. But, without warning, firefighters can be expected to help with a daring rescue that puts their own lives in jeopardy.

That's exactly what happened on April 30, 1906, under the Milwaukee River.

Six men — Tom O'Donnell, James Zymom, Thomas Blackwell, Martin Kotouski, Tom Jennings and Jacob Flejter — were working 70 feet under the river that Monday on a project that was far behind schedule. The tunnel would carry water lines and electrical cable and was supposed to be completed the day before.

A crowd gathers at the scene of the tunnel collapse.

The men had reached the center of the river, about two hundred feet from the tunnel opening. An air lock with heavy steel doors at each end helped keep sand, mud and water out of the tunnel. Air pressure was maintained at sixteen pounds per square inch. The M.H. McGovern Construction Co. of Chicago had a $20,000 contract to build the tunnel starting at the foot of Knap Street.

About 11 a.m., the sand above the men began to collapse, filling the tunnel with water and mud. The men scrambled back as quickly as possible toward the safety of the air lock. They swung open the heavy door and plunged inside as the 620-pound door slammed shut behind them.

The men had fled the tunnel in the nick of time as they heard the mud and water pouring in. But only five men made it through the door before it closed.

Flejter tripped over a mud-slick board and those few lost seconds trapped him like a rat in a maze.

Flejter, age 30, was a German immigrant who had served in the militia before coming to the United States. A single man, he lived with his brother at 1010 Midland Ave.

Within three minutes, the water and mud had reached Flejter's chin. He held his head high to keep it above the water level as he alternately pounded on the door and tried to yank it open. Finally, he put his fist through a small bull's-eye-shaped window, shattering the glass. Mud and water poured into the air lock. Besides the water and mud swirling around him in the darkness, wooden planks floated on top, occasionally banging Flejter in the head.

"I just stood there and fought the planks that kept pounding me," he later told the *Milwaukee Sentinel.* "Then, I broke the glass in the door and the water began rushing through."

When firefighters arrived at the air lock, it was rapidly filling with water. They quickly set up three hoses to a fire boat above them to pump out the sludge. Working waist-deep in mud, three men hurled themselves against the door but it wouldn't budge.

"For God's sake, save me!" Flejter shouted in a thick German accent through the small window. "Don't leave me here to die like a drowned rat!"

"Keep your head," admonished fire Capt. Peter Lancaster. "We are doing all that we can to save you."

Besides Lancaster, Capt. Harris Giddings and Assistant Chief Lawrence Hanlon also were in the tunnel, risking their lives in a desperate effort to rescue Flejter. Through the small window, they passed a crowbar to Flejter so he could pry the door from his side as they kept trying to open it.

Above ground, Mayor Becker arrived to monitor the rescue. He called for divers to try to plug the tunnel leak with bags of cement but no divers were available. The mayor considered bringing in boilermakers to cut a hole in the door with torches.

Meanwhile, the firefighters continued to work at opening the door. Pumping out the mud and water stabilized the level so that it had stopped rising. Despite their best efforts, however, the door remained firmly closed one-and-a-half hours after the cave-in at 12:30 p.m.

To bolster Flejter's sagging spirits, they tried to pass him a flask of whiskey but the flask wouldn't fit through the opening. They poured some whiskey into a soda bottle and passed it through. But Flejter wouldn't drink it. Later, he said that he honored a farewell promise made to his mother before leaving Germany that he wouldn't drink alcohol again.

Inch by inch, the valiant firefighters finally were able to open the door but it was slow, tedious work. Finally, they got it opened enough to pass a shovel through the Flejter.

He worked furiously, seemingly with a second wind, moving as much mud as he could from his side of the door. As he dug, the firefighters continued to push. The door jerked opened in tiny increments until it opened enough for the trapped man to squeeze through the opening.

Flejter had spent two hours and fifteen minutes trapped in the tunnel but, to him, it had seemed an eternity. His face was white as a sheet and he was covered with mud from head to toe as he finally was brought out of the tunnel.

Lancaster, Giddings and Hanlon each received $1,500 and a bronze medal from the Carnegie Hero Fund Commission in recognition of the fact that they risked their own lives to save Flejter. As for Flejter, he went home after a night in the hospital and said he had enough of tunnel work.

"I was getting pretty good wages at the work but no more of it for me," he told a *Sentinel* reporter. "I am going to make my living on top of the ground after this."

Chapter 22

Civil rights pioneer
Hilton Hanna

When a ship came in to port at Matthew Town, Hilton Hanna and the other boys would swarm around the crew, asking questions about foreign lands. One particular captain once lived in Green Bay and he told the boys about a northern paradise called Wisconsin. For these Bahamian boys, the ships were their exotic window to the rest of the world.

Young Hilton Hanna might have set his sights on Oxford or Cambridge universities in England for Matthew Town was then controlled by the British. Instead, he hoped someday to visit this place called Wisconsin that was so touted by Captain McLaughlin.

Hanna's parents had died when he was very young and, at age 14, he came to Florida with an aunt and uncle to work picking fruits and vegetables.

At Tuskegee Institute, Hanna learned the printing

trade. Among his Sunday school teachers was George Washington Carver, the famous African-American scientist. Later, he received a bachelor's degree in English at Talladega College in Alabama.

During the Depression years, he worked as a reporter for the *Atlanta World*, a black newspaper, and volunteered at the Atlanta public library. Hanna organized his first worker education classes, hoping to offset low morale and bitterness due to high levels of unemployment.

In 1934, Hanna came north, enrolling at the University of Wisconsin in Madison, where he pursued a post-graduate degree in economics. Tuition for out-of-state students was $137 a semester, which he could not afford easily. He would alternate going to school for a semester and then taking off the following semester to work full-time and save money. He wrote a column and editorials for the Daily Cardinal, a student newspaper, and joined the varsity debate team. He was the first University of Wisconsin African-American elected to the national forensics fraternity.

During his semesters off, he cooked, washed dishes and waited on tables. He also worked in the casing department at Oscar Mayer, where he became chairman of the union education committee of Butchermen's Local 538.

Using his ingenuity, Hanna financed a trip to Europe in 1936 by a speaking tour of schools and clubs. With eleven other graduate students, teachers and social workers, he visited England, Scandinavia, Germany, Russia and Poland.

Madison Newspapers Inc. newsroom library

Hilton Hanna signs a copy of his book for the Rev. Martin Luther King Jr. in 1961.

As a boy in the Bahamas, Hanna hadn't experienced racial discrimination. But he quickly became aware of it in the United States. In a 1943 guest editorial in the *Wisconsin State Journal,* he described social conditions that would persist for decades: "The Negro is again expected to wait in line for the crumbs that fall from the table of opportunity," he wrote. "It is as true today as ever that he is the last hired and the first fired."

With Harry and Velma Hamilton and Hazel and Odell Taliaferro, Hanna worked to revive the Madison chapter of the National Association for the Advancement of Colored People (NAACP).

"When we put it together, Velma Hamilton was president and I was secretary," he said much later. "We didn't have to wait for women's liberation to give authority to competent women."

During the war, Hanna also fought for equal recreational opportunities for African-American soldiers.

"If it took the problems of the USO and entertainment for the Negro soldiers to awaken our citizens, white and colored, to the possiblities for organization for providing opportunities for the Negro, the ill wind of dissension will have served a purpose," he wrote.

In Madison, Hanna wrote radio scripts and worked as a masseur at the YMCA. By the early 1950s, he had become a union educational adviser and he was invited by the U.S. State Department to tour Latin America. He found a hostile reception, especially from Communists.

"They were amazed that the U.S. government had sent a Negro as its representative," he said after the trip. "I believe I was able to correct a distorted picture they have of racial prejudice in the U.S. We in the U.S. have failed to tell our story. So the Communists, who are much in the minority in Latin America, have been able to get control."

During the 1950s, Hanna lived for a short time in Chicago. But he moved back to Madison and, in 1968, he was elected president of the Madison Urban League, resurrecting that organization as he had done twenty years earlier with the NAACP chapter.

Hanna is the author of *Picket and the Pen,* a history of the union that has been used as a college textbook on collective bargaining. In 1972, he was elected international vice president of his union, which later became the United Food and Commercial Workers Union. After his retirement in 1978, Hanna became active in the Order of the Eastern Star.

Hilton Hanna is one of Wisconsin's most learned and outspoken advocates for social change. He is a world traveler, educator and union leader who spoke out against racism and social injustice long before the freedom rides and desegregation orders of the 1950s. Sadly, in a 1988 interview, Hanna said he didn't believe much had changed.

"So far as blacks in general in this community, they've been ignored," he said. "The socio-economic condition is not much different than when I arrived here in 1934. You still have problems with racism and that goes for jobs, kids in school and all the rest of it."

Chapter 23

They call him Crazy Legs
Elroy Hirsch

T hey called him the Whiz from Wausau. Or the
Ghost. But, mostly, they knew him as Crazy
Legs.

Elroy "Crazy Legs" Hirsch was a sensation in Wisconsin athletics during the mid-1940s, even though
he played just one year on the Badger football squad.
But what a year it was.

The 1942 team was dubbed the best fielded by the
University of Wisconsin since 1912. Led by left halfback Hirsch, fullback Pat Harder and right halfback
Mark Hoskins, the team won eight games, tied one
and lost one to finish second in the Big Ten Conference. Hirsch, nicknamed the Ghost for his prowess as
a breakaway runner, was fifth in the Big Ten Conference in total offense, third in rushing with an average
of 64.6 yards per game and seventh in passing. Not

bad for a sophomore.

Those numbers promised even greater things the following year but it wasn't to be. Hirsch was ordered to join the Marine Corps Reserve at the University of Michigan in Ann Arbor the following year.

The numbers alone don't convey the excitement generated by Hirsch's performance. In nearly every Badger victory during the 1942 season, it was a long run by Hirsch that made the difference. His fifty-yard run won a game against a military team and another dramatic thirty-five-yard run earned a tie with Notre Dame. A twenty-yard run contributed to a 35-7 victory over Marquette University. Against the University of Missouri, he carried the ball 22 times, gained 174 yards and scored two touchdowns in a 17-9 victory. A sixty-two-yard run contributed to a 13-7 victory over Great Lakes Naval Training Center and he scored

Madison Newspapers Inc. newsroom library

Elroy "Crazylegs" Hirsch

Wisconsin's first touchdown in a 13-7 win over Purdue University.

Besides his skill as a runner, Hirsch's unusual style also contributed to the performance.

"Hirsch ran like a demented duck," a Chicago sports reporter wrote after the Great Lakes game. "His crazy legs were gyrating in six different directions all at the same time."

Back in Wausau, Hirsch had a difficult time making the high school football team. The coach thought he was too small. But Hirsch was hailed as one of the greatest prep athletes ever in the Wisconsin Valley League. Besides football, he also starred in basketball, baseball and track. In his final game with Wausau, Hirsch scored five touchdowns and passed for another score in a 45-12 victory over Merrill.

In 1943, Badger fans viewed Hirsch as a Wisconsin player "on loan" to Michigan during his military service. As a loaner player, Hirsch not only starred in football, he also earned letters in basketball, baseball and track. He played center on the basketball team, then went on to star in the high jump and broad jump for the track team. In baseball, he pitched a one-hitter against Ohio State. By early June 1944, Hirsch admitted to a newspaper columnist that he was tired.

Later that month, however, he returned to Madison to play baseball in a benefit game to raise money for war bonds. In typical Hirsch style, he clouted a grand slam home run in the fifth inning.

"Elroy 'Crazy Legs' Hirsch is a 'money' performer in athletics if ever there was one," wrote Henry

McCormick in the *Wisconsin State Journal.* "More re-
markable than Hirsch's clutch effort to my way of
thinking was the widespread belief among spectators
that Hirsch would handle the situation in spectacular
fashion."

Everyone hoped that Hirsch would return to Wisconsin to finish his glorious college career that began
in 1942. Instead, he played for a California team the
following year and then signed a professional contract
with the Chicago Rockets.

Before turning pro, Hirsch turned in a final stellar
amateur performance during the College All-Star game
in August 1946, scoring two touchdowns to lead the
All-Stars to a 16-0 upset victory over the Los Angeles
Rams. Two months earlier, Hirsch had married Ruth
Katherine Stahmer, his high-school sweetheart.

Despite Hirsch's presence, the Rockets had difficulty drawing fans. "They used to call up and ask
what time the game started," Hirsch later recalled.
"We asked, 'What time would you like to come?'"

Until 1948, Elroy Hirsch was a star athlete but not
a true hero. Something happened that year, however,
that propelled the crazy legs runner to heroic status.
During a Chicago Rockets game, he suffered a severe
skull fracture. Doctors told him he would never play
football again.

But Hirsch wouldn't accept that diagnosis. Just as
he had battled against would-be tacklers, he fought
back, slowly regaining his strength. He was back on
the field the following year as a halfback for the Los
Angeles Rams. In 1951, he starred on the world cham-

pion Rams team, setting a National Football League record of 1,495 yards on 66 pass receptions. He tied another record of 17 touchdown passes caught that year.

Hirsch's personal struggle to play again after his injury inspired a 1953 movie called *Crazy Legs* and the former Wisconsin athlete also starred in two other films, *Unchained* in 1955 and *Zero Hour* in 1957. But Hirsch found making passes at screen idols more difficult than catching them on the football field.

"Nothing is tougher than kissing a girl with the movie crew standing around gawking," he said in 1957. "I pay for those romantic scenes on the football field. There's an awful lot of needling out there during a game."

Although a movie career wasn't in his future, Hirsch retired from football in 1957 and took a public relations job with Union Oil Co. But he couldn't stay away from the game and soon returned to the Rams as general manager.

Throughout his career, Wisconsin always claimed Hirsch as its own, even though he played just a single season for the Badgers. In 1969, Hirsch was given a hero's welcome as he returned to Madison to take the job as university athletic director.

But Hirsch's eighteen-year tenure as athletic director wasn't as successful as his football career. Although other Badger teams won championships, football victories were scarce and fans could only reminisce about the 1963 Rose Bowl team. Hirsch retired in 1987, five years before Wisconsin returned once again to the Rose

Bowl. These days, the trim former star and athletic director with a trademark flat-top haircut still lives in Madison. He is remembered each spring in Madison during a Crazy Legs run for charity. A street near the stadium also is named Crazylegs Lane.

Chapter 24

To kill a Communist

Ralph Sacks

The 17-year-old boy didn't attract much attention at first from Ralph Sacks and Fred Bassett Blair. The two men stood across the counter from each other when the boy — blond, about five-feet, eight-inches tall and weighing 165 pounds — came into Mary's Bookstore in Milwaukee about 1 p.m. on November 28, 1966.

"Can I help you?" Blair asked.

"No, I just want to look around," the boy said. Then he began browsing through newspapers and books.

A moment later, he turned back to Blair.

"Are you Mr. Blair?"

"Yes."

The boy began pulling a gun from his coat pocket but it caught on the lining.

Madison Newspapers Inc. newsroom library

**Fred Bassett Blair speaks at a rally during his 1966
campaign for governor.**

"I'm going to get me a Commie before I die."

But it wouldn't happen. Sacks watched the boy
struggling to get the gun out of his pocket. Blair ducked
behind the counter as the boy fired at him, but missed.
Sacks lunged at the boy, grabbing his shoulder and
wrist. The boy fired again three times and, this time,
two bullets passed through Sacks' right arm.

Although he was wounded, Sacks persisted. He grabbed the boy's wrist and forced his arm upward. He tried to break the boy's grip on the gun and wrestled the assailant into an alcove. Meanwhile, Blair had grabbed a toy baseball bat and come up behind the boy. Blair slammed the toy bat hard down on the boy's head and Sacks was able to grab the pistol.

"I give up," the boy said.

While Blair guarded the youth, Sacks ran to a nearby smoke shop to summon the police. Blair asked the boy who had put him up to it.

"Nobody sent me," the boy said. "It was all my own idea. You're a Communist. I want to kill a Communist."

The boy also begged Blair to shoot him.

"I want to die," he said. "I wanted to commit suicide but didn't have enough nerve. You can say it was self-defense."

The violence against Blair culminated nearly a half century of hatred for the state's leading Communist. Three weeks earlier, Blair, a party member for 40 years, had run as a write-in candidate for governor.

Blair's first run for governor came in 1942, during the heat of World War II. That year, Wisconsin Secretary of State Fred Zimmerman refused to remove Blair's name from the ballot despite the threat of lawsuits. A year earlier, the Legislature had passed the Gettelman Law, which barred recognition of parties affiliated with the U.S. Communist Party. Blair ran as an Independent Communist.

Four years later, Blair ran again. The Soviet Union

had turned from a wartime ally into a post-war foe. Claire Merten, a Milwaukee notary public, resigned his commission in protest that Blair's wife, Elizabeth, also had been appointed a notary public.

"I am devoting my life to a fight against communism, fascism and racial prejudice, and therefore will have nothing in common with either communists or communist sympathizers even as an ordinary notary public," Merten wrote in a letter to Gov. Goodland.

In 1961, an illegal wiretap was found on Blair's phone. The following year, he wrote about the problems he faced over his political beliefs. "When Communists can run their own candidates without repression and intimidation like every other political party, then professional anti-Communists won't be able to draw the red herring across the voters' trail to obscure the real issues of taxation, bigotry, Birchism and bossism," Blair wrote in a letter published in the Madison *Capital Times*.

In 1965, FBI director J. Edgar Hoover had identified Mary's Bookstore as one of eight "major Communist bookstores operating in the United States at this time." The following year, Blair mounted his first campaign for governor in twenty years, although he also ran for the U.S. Senate, Congress and Milwaukee mayor.

"I am running to help open doors for the people to forge a movement of the two old parties — a movement that will in the near future give the people an alternative to the Democratic and Republican parties," Blair said in announcing his 1966 candidacy. In September, he brought his campaign to Beloit College as a speaker at a student-sponsored lecture series. In October, a meeting sponsored by Blair at Jefferson Hall in Milwaukee was moved from the hall to his home after telephone threats.

Blair's high profile that year may have sparked the attempt to assassinate him. Naturally, Blair equated the attempt with the Vietnam War: "It's part of the whole general pattern. On account of Johnson's war on Vietnam, they feel that if they can kill Communists in Vietnam, they can kill Communists here."

A psychiatric exam was ordered for the 17-year-old boy. Sacks, an Air Force veteran and father of one child, received a bronze medal and $1,100 in cash from the Carnegie Hero Fund Commission. He said he was surprised that the boy had remained so calm throughout the incident.

Blair said he was surprised that Sacks acted so quickly. "Ralph is such a mild guy usually that I never thought he could have done it," Blair told the *Milwaukee Journal.*

A month after the shooting, Blair wrote letters to Wisconsin newspapers seeking contributions for Sacks, who missed several weeks of work while recovering from his wounds.

"At a time when there is cause to be concerned about people not coming to the help of each other — an example of heroism like Ralph's should be applauded and aided," Blair wrote. "Would you help me give substantive aid to someone who not only saved my life — but acted in the best tradition of mutual aid?"

Blair finally got on the gubernatorial ballot again in 1974 but that success didn't mean much in terms of vote totals. His running mate that year was his second wife, Mary. By that time, the bookstore named after her was no longer in business, although Blair still sold books by mail order.

Blair's rhetoric and the hatred of him may seem pointless to some today, now that Communist regimes have collapsed in the Soviet Union and Eastern Europe. At the time, however, the rhetoric was taken seriously, even though Blair rarely drew more than a handful of votes in his campaigns.

In 1961, the *Wisconsin State Journal* captured the prevailing attitude in an editorial supporting national registration of communists:

"It is not an independent party. It is not American, it is not loyal. It is a conspiracy manipulated from the Moscow headquarters of freedom's greatest enemy, and largely financed by the same source."

If American communists like Blair truly were financed and controlled by Moscow, then history shows the scheme clearly was underfunded and bungled. And Sacks is one of Wisconsin's heroes not because of who he saved but because he put his own life in jeopardy for someone else.

Chapter 25

Radical hero
James Groppi

To many people, the Rev. James Groppi was far from a hero. He won no military medals. He literally saved no lives. He was a radical priest during the turbulent 1960s who led marches for open housing in Milwaukee as well as a controversial takeover of the Wisconsin Assembly. Although thirty years ago he was among the most unpopular men in Wisconsin, Groppi was a catalyst for change. He went to jail for his convictions and the open housing for which he fought has long been the law.

Groppi was born November 16, 1931, in an Italian neighborhood called Bay View on Milwaukee's South Side. His father was an Italian immigrant who ran a small grocery store and had nine children, four sons and five daughters.

The younger Groppi played basketball in high

school but, during the summer, he worked at a youth center on the city's predominantly black North Side. Working at the youth center was his awakening to the extreme poverty and obstacles faced by African-American families.

Groppi attended St. Francis Seminary and was ordained as a Roman Catholic priest in 1960, during the height of the civil rights marches and restaurant sit-ins throughout the South.

It may be difficult for us to imagine today the seething tension of the 1960s — between black and white, young and old, pro-war and anti-war sympathizers. Some of the young people pouring into the streets to protest social injustice were perhaps motivated by a naive idealism in that era when the nation still appeared to have a conscience that could be influenced by its citizenry.

After becoming a priest, Groppi was assigned to St. Boniface parish on the North Side. His interest in working with young people forged during those high school summers blossomed and he organized a youth council of the National Association for the Advancement of Colored People (NAACP). He also went South, where he participated in civil rights demonstrations.

In October 1965, Groppi led a massive boycott of Milwaukee's public schools to protest their racial imbalance. As many as ten percent of the district's 122,000 students stayed home during the boycott. Groppi was ordered to stop promoting the boycott and he obeyed.

The following year, Groppi attacked Circuit Judge

Robert C. Cannon. Although Cannon was generally regarded as a liberal judge, he was criticized for being a member of the Fraternal Order of Eagles, which barred African-Americans from joining. He was elected circuit judge in 1945, at age 28, the youngest judge ever to serve in a Wisconsin court. Cannon's father was Raymond Cannon, an attorney who had served in Congress and represented some members of the notorious Black Sox baseball team 50 years earlier.

"Get off the bench or get out of the club," Groppi and his followers told the judge.

"I came from an Italian ghetto," Groppi said. "I'm committed to work in a Negro ghetto. My parish work is different than the kind I would do in Judge Cannon's parish. My parish is actually a mission and we have to be missionaries."

This time, Archbishop William Cousins didn't order Groppi to stop demonstrating against Judge Cannon, although the archbishop said the demonstrations might be ill-conceived. "They can picket until doomsday," Cannon said. "I'm not changing my mind."

Groppi was one of few white men of the era who won unchallenged respect from his black congregation. "No one has the power that he has over the kids in the neighborhood," said neighborhood activist Alberta Harris.

By 1967, riots had broken out in inner-city black neighborhoods across America. In Milwaukee, a riot lasted just a few hours in July before National Guard troops moved in to quell it. Groppi attacked the police as trigger happy because they shot and killed

Madison Newspapers Inc. newsroom library

James Groppi during the Assembly takeover.

Clifford McKissick as he ran from the scene of a firebombing.

In August of that year, Groppi began leading black marchers to the all-white South Side in support of open housing. In one demonstration, the marchers held a picnic in Kosciusko Park, where they were jeered by a mob of two thousand whites. Rocks and bottles were thrown at Groppi and his two-hundred-fifty demonstrators. Wearing riot helmets and armed with rifles, police dispersed a group of about a hundred white protesters. On August 30, the black marchers returned after another South Side confrontation with whites to find their headquarters, called Freedom House, burned to the ground.

For over a month, Groppi led the open housing protest. Judge Christ Seraphim was sitting on his porch on Labor Day weekend when demonstrators streamed past. Like Cannon, Seraphim was another liberal judge who belonged to the all-white Eagles Club.

The marchers visited the City Council, where they chanted: "We don't want any committees. We don't want any discussions. We don't want any delays. We want that bill signed."

A policeman called Groppi a "white nigger." Groppi responded that it was the nicest thing he had been called in a week. A bridge to the South Side was dubbed Milwaukee's Mason-Dixon line.

When Mayor Henry Maier banned night demonstrations, Groppi promptly disobeyed the order. More than four hundred protesters were met by tear gas and police officers swinging nightsticks. Several demonstrators and three police officers were injured in the melee.

Groppi predicted further violence if conditions didn't change. To many people, he himself was the instigator of violence. In reality, he may have provided a way for the African-American community to vent its anger peacefully.

Maier blasted Groppi for helping encourage a racial imbalance in the suburbs by focusing his efforts on the inner city. But an open housing ordinance was passed the following year. Fifteen suburban communities also passed open housing ordinances and six Milwaukee alderman were replaced as a result of the marches.

Passage of the open housing law, however, didn't end Groppi's career as an activist and demonstrator. In 1969, he and about a thousand protesters stormed the

State Capitol and took over the Assembly chambers for half a day to protest welfare cuts. Groppi was arrested for disorderly conduct and found in contempt of the Legislature under a 121-year-old law that had never been used. The contempt citation ultimately was overturned after the priest spent time in the Dane County Jail.

By the 1970s, the civil rights era had faded and Groppi turned his attention to the peace movement and the battle of Native Americans. For awhile, he drove a cab to support himself and went to law school.

In 1976, he challenged the celibacy rule for priests by marrying Peggy Rozga, who taught English at the University of Wisconsin-Milwaukee. He was promptly excommunicated and applied for a job as a bus driver.

As the Reagan era dawned, Groppi predicted a return of 1960s-style activism. "The rich eat cake and spend $200,000 on new china in the White House while poor children eat catsup instead of vegetables," he said. "I think Reagan is going to put all us old activists back on the streets."

But it was not to be. In 1983, after a tie vote, Groppi won a coin toss to become president of the transit workers' union. The following year, he had surgery to remove a brain tumor. Groppi died on November 4, 1985, leaving behind his widow and two daughters, Christine and Anna, ages 4 and 6.

After his death, Groppi finally achieved recognition for his civil rights efforts. The 16th Street Bridge, where he led his marchers to the South Side, was renamed in his honor. In 1987, about four-hundred-fifty people gathered to retrace the steps of the open housing marches 20 years earlier.

The impact of James Groppi, a controversial figure, is difficult to measure. Although poverty and racial segregation of Milwaukee's North Side remains, open housing is now the law. Instead of demonstrators, landlords who discriminate now are met by swift justice.

Chapter 26

Wisconsin's Rockefeller
James H. Stout

J ames H. Stout wasn't a Wisconsin hero because he
saved a life. He wasn't a great athlete or warrior.
Stout attained heroic status because he changed the
face of American education at the turn of the 20th
Century.

Stout was born in 1848 at Dubuque, Iowa. His
father, Henry L. Stout, ran a forest products business,
benefiting immensely from the logging era that swept
Wisconsin during the late 19th Century. After graduating from the University of Chicago, James Stout
returned to Dubuque to join his father's flourishing
lumber business.

Under his father's tutelage, Stout learned every as-
pect of the lumber business from stacking boards prop-
erly in the yards to supervising the rafting of rough
timber down the Mississippi River. After buying out

another lumber company, Henry Stout managed Knapp, Stout & Co., one of the most successful lumbering businesses of the time.

As his position grew in his father's business, James Stout became active in community affairs, serving on the boards of the public library and hospital association. By 1880, however, the younger Stout had moved to St. Louis to supervise the business operations in that city.

At the 1876 Centennial Exposition in Philadelphia, several European exhibitors demonstrated a new direction in higher education. They had begun programs to teach technical skills instead of the standard liberal arts education. These programs combined industrial arts and home economics. St. Louis became the first large city in America to establish a technical education program and, as a business leader, Stout became vitally interested in it. When he overheard a worker complain that he was too poor to send his three sons to the new technical school, he offered to provide the money, only the first of his many educational grants.

But it wasn't until James Stout moved to Menomonie, in 1889, that he became truly dedicated to technical education. In 1890, he built a two-room school that offered industrial arts and home economics courses. Similar courses soon were adopted by the Menomonie public schools. The small school attracted so many students that Stout built a $100,000, three-story building to house the Stout Institute. That building was destroyed by fire four years later but Stout quickly had it rebuilt.

Stout's bold educational experiment attracted national attention and other communities scrambled for the few available technical education instructors. He married Angeline Wilson in 1899. She was the daughter of Capt. William Wilson, one of the founders of Knapp, Stout & Co. In 1903, the focus of the Menomonie technical school was changed to educate teachers of kindergarten, industrial arts and home economics. Stout Institute became the first teacher-training college in America for technical education.

Despite the national acclaim, it wasn't until 1917 that the Legislature finally recog-

State Historical Society of Wisconsin
James Stout

nized Stout Institute as an educational institution. The course of study was extended to four years and the institute was permitted to award degrees.

Stout served as a state senator from 1894 until his

death in 1910, during Wisconsin government's Golden
Age. Many of his educational concepts became part of
what become known as the "Wisconsin Idea," championed by Gov. Robert M. La Follette.

As chairman of the Senate Committee on Education, Stout initiated the state's first traveling library
system. Before smaller communities had their own libraries, the traveling library shipped the latest books
from one community to the next in boxes of fifty to
seventy-five books. By the 1930s, more than sixty thousand volumes were circulating around the state in five
hundred boxes. The traveling library survives today as
a network of state library systems. Stout also chaired
the Free Library Commission, which promoted setting up libraries in many communities, as well as a
commission that built the Wisconsin Historical Library.

But Stout's vision and philanthropy weren't limited
to education and libraries. He built one of the first
modern highways near Menomonie and sponsored park
and playground legislation. Stout Institute became
Stout State College in 1955 and, later, was incorpo-
rated into Wisconsin's state university system as the
University of Wisconsin-Stout.

Stout comes closest to Wisconsin's own version of
David Rockefeller. He was a founding father of technical education in America but his public service made
him a true Wisconsin hero.

Chapter 27

Taming Shorty
Donald Sweetland

T here are an excess of opportunities for heroism on Wisconsin's many farms throughout the state. True courage often has been demonstrated in equipment accidents. In some cases, brave men and women have gone in to rescue someone buried in grain or silage only to die themselves.

Fourteen-year-old Donald Sweetland was a farmyard hero on February 4, 1950. On Saturdays, Donald often helped his cousin, Jesse Biegemann, age 21, clean out the barn on the Biegemann's farm near Genesse in Waukesha County. He didn't really like to be around Shorty but he knew the routine. Shorty was a bull.

Donald usually helped his cousin put the cows and bulls in the barnyard, then tackled the task of removing piles of manure from the stalls. The manure was taken by wheelbarrow to a cart attached to a tractor. It was slow, tedious work, taking a couple of hours. When the boys were finished, Donald knew it was his job to haul away the manure wagon while Jess led the animals back into the barn. On this chilly February day, Donald drove away in the wagon.

Jesse led the cows to their stalls, then returned for Shorty as he always did. This time, however, Shorty got angry, possibly because Jesse was carrying a pitchfork. The bull suddenly charged, breaking the pitchfork and flipping Jesse in air. After tossing the young man twice, the bull pinned him to the ground with its horns. Fortunately, the horns were on either side of Jesse's chest.

What the bull would have done next will never be known. A dazed Jesse lay on the ground, still gripping the ring in the bull's nose. Would the bull have left Jesse alone? Or would the animal have tossed Jesse again, perhaps finishing him off?

At that point, Donald drove around the corner of the barn. "I stopped the tractor, jumped off and climbed a four-foot concrete wall that enclosed the barnyard," he said. "For just a minute, I stopped to think."

Donald was afraid of the bull and didn't want to go near it. But he knew that his cousin could be seriously injured if he didn't intervene. Donald walked over to the bull. He pried Jesse's fingers off the ring, then tugged at the bull.

Slowly, Donald walked backward fifty feet to the barn doorway and then back another twenty to the bullpen. Amazingly, Shorty followed Donald without resistance. Donald got the bull inside the pen, closed the gate and ran to the house. He asked Biegemann's wife to call an ambulance. Jesse was taken to Waukesha Memorial Hospital, where he was treated for dozens of bruises. It took him two months to recover from his injuries.

Donald Sweetland was awarded a bronze medal and $250 from the Carnegie Hero Fund Commission for his bravery in saving his cousin from potential serious injury.

The incident and the award, however, didn't diminish Donald's fear of bulls. How did he overcome his fear to save his cousin?

"I didn't have time to be scared," he said afterward.

Sweetland later married and moved to Texas, settling near Houston. He died in 1990, according to his cousin, David Sweetland, who still lives in Waukesha County.

Chapter 28

A master showman
Al Ringling

B araboo is a small city with a funny name. Not far from Wisconsin Dells, the Wisconsin River and Devil's Lake State Park, it is one of Wisconsin's most popular tourist destinations in the summer.

Beautiful homes are perched on the bluffs on the north side of town. The courthouse square has a quaint small-town feel that moviemakers relished in the 1994 film, *I Love Trouble*. Most important of all, however, Baraboo is a name that seems synonymous with circus. It is the home of the Circus World Museum — a tribute to an ambitious family of five brothers who built the Greatest Show on Earth.

Perhaps it was a stern family upbringing that caused Al Ringling and his four brothers to become fascinated with the circus. Their parents, August and Salome Ruengling were strict Lutherans who believed that circus people were evil.

Like a roving circus troupe, the Ruengling family moved around quite often. August and Salome were married in Milwaukee. They lived in Chicago, then moved to Baraboo. During the Civil War, the family fared well but, afterward, an economic crash devastated the family's finances and they moved to McGregor, Iowa.

McGregor is across the river from Prairie du Chien, where entertainment used to arrive by Mississippi River boat during the post-war years. Ringling and his brothers went to the dock to watch the arrival of the Dan Rice show. The boys watched open-mouthed as an elephant came down the gangplank. Later, the circus strongman visited their father's harness shop to have a strap repaired.

The boys were hooked. After moving back to Baraboo, Al practiced juggling plates while John learned to sing and dance. Alf T. and Charles learned musical instruments while Otto planned pin games for neighborhood children.

After several neighborhood performances in Baraboo, the Ringling boys decided to take their show on the road. Al took $3.75 from his savings to print handbills and a performance was scheduled in a nearby village. The show drew an audience of 47 and the boys began planning a more ambitious tour. In November 1882, the boys traveled to Mazomanie for their first road performance as the Ringling Brothers Classic and Comic Concert Company.

"I was never again to be as uneasy as on this first

appearance," Al said much later. "We had gone far enough from Baraboo that no one would know us. On the afternoon of the day of the show we paraded the streets. There were fifty-nine paid admissions to the performance, enough to meet the hotel expenses and have a little left over."

With Al in blackface, Alf T. playing drums and Charles on trombone, the brothers toured Iowa and the Dakotas before returning to Wisconsin to close the season at Oregon in Dane County. They had earned $300, more than their father's harness shop income, and also had bought new clothes.

With the money from their successful tour, the brothers bought a monkey and a hyena and started their first real circus in 1884. The boys toured most of the year and established winter quarters in their

Madison Newspapers Inc. newsroom library

Al Ringling performs with a troupe of trained dogs in this 1887 photo.

hometown of Baraboo. Their most dramatic act featured Alf as "the man with an iron jaw," balancing a farm plow on his chin. The proceeds went to buying more animals and making their show bigger and better. By 1888, the circus had two elephants and a band. Al served as ringmaster before performing in a cannonball act. The circus now was grossing $15,000 a year.

Four years later, the Ringling Brothers Circus rolled into Milwaukee in eighteen rail cars. Besides the usual elephants and monkeys, the show also featured two hippopotami. In Milwaukee, the Ringling circus went head-to-head against a larger rival: Barnum & Bailey. The Ringling show was standing-room-only.

In 1908, the Ringling Brothers bought out Barnum & Bailey for $410,000. The Barnum & Bailey circus was operated independently for a decade until 1919, when the two circuses merged into what was dubbed the Greatest Show on Earth.

A key to the phenomenal success of the Ringling Brothers was their creativity. As the circus grew, the humble little musical band was supplanted by pageants highlighting biblical, historical or mythical figures such as Solomon, Joan of Arc or Cinderella.

Despite their worldwide travels and successful barnstorming tours throughout the nation, Baraboo remained home to the Ringlings. Al Ringling built a $135,000 house in 1909 and opened the Al Ringling Theatre in 1915.

But the circus moved out of Baraboo after the merger with Barnum & Bailey and the combined circus wintered in Connecticut.

The giant circus returned to Baraboo in 1933 for a special tribute. Elephants appeared in gold paint and more than 40,000 people gathered for the first Ringling hometown performance in over 35 years. By this time, John was the last living brother. Otto had died in 1911, Al in 1916, Alf in 1919 and Charles in 1926.

Besides their worldwide contribution to the circus, the Ringling brothers also were the first of Wisconsin's master showmen. In recent years, this tradition has been carried on by Tommy Bartlett of Wisconsin Dells and Alex Jordan, developer of the House on the Rock.

Chapter 29

A babysitter earns her money

Sharon Boero

Wisconsin's most famous babysitting crime was the disappearance of Evelyn Hartley from the La Crosse home of Professor Viggio Rasmussen in 1953. Evelyn's body never was found and the case remains unsolved.

Sixteen-year-old Sharon Boero faced a similar life-threatening situation on Feb. 9, 1958, while she was babysitting for the children of Robert Everson at their Strum, Wisconsin farmhouse.

The Eversons, who had gone out to Independence for the evening, operated the Chimney Rock store and lived in an attached residence. The family's four children and a step-child were upstairs asleep about midnight when the smell of smoke awakened Sharon, who was napping on the living room couch. When Sharon smelled smoke, she ran to the telephone and tried to call for help but the line was dead. She ran upstairs and awakened the children to get them out of the house. Sharon scooped up one-year-old Ellen in her arms and told the other children to follow her. But when she got downstairs, Sharon saw that only Peggy, age 8, had done as she had asked.

Marie, age 9, broke a window and went out with Ronald, age 7, on to a porch roof. Marie escaped by sliding down a drain pipe but Ronald went back to bed.

Although flames now were licking near the staircase, the babysitter left the youngest child with her sister and fought her way through the heat and smoke to go back upstairs. She picked up Virginia, age 5, and told Ronald to come with her. Braving six-foot flames that were burning the lower steps, Sharon got to the ground floor, then ran beneath flames that were burning the ceiling to the outside. She and Virginia were seriously burned. When she got outside, the babysitter saw that Ronald had remained inside.

While Sharon headed for the nearest farmhouse with the children, she met Bernard Colby, age 46, on the road. Colby, who had asthma, was driving home with his family. When he heard about Ronald's plight, Colby drove to the Everson farmhouse but the flames were too high for him to enter by the front door. He drove back to his farm for a ladder, then returned to the Everson house.

Colby went up the ladder to the kitchen roof and broke the window to Ronald's room. Closing his eyes and holding his breath, Colby climbed into the room and groped around for the boy. He returned to the roof for a gulp for fresh air, then went back inside and found the boy, who was unconscious. Colby carried Ronald out the window and down the ladder, minutes before the flames broke through the roof and outer walls.

Another passing motorist, Ralph Bautch, drove to the fire department to report the blaze. Firefighters were unable to bring the fire under control and it destroyed the frame building. The loss was estimated at $15,000.

Ronald was taken to the hospital and was revived. Virginia had to be hospitalized for three weeks. Sharon Boero, the courageous babysitter, recovered in two months but had permanent scars on both hands.

For her rescue of the Everson children, Sharon Boero was awarded a bronze medal from the Carnegie Hero Fund Commission and $250 for educational or other purposes.

Chapter 30

Woman of the century

Golda Meir

G olda Meir, the first woman prime minister of Israel, was a citizen of the world but her roots were in Milwaukee.

She was born May 3, 1898, in Kiev, Russia to Moshe Mabovich, a carpenter, and his wife, Bluma. In Russia, the Mabovich family, including their three daughters, suffered under anti-semitic laws as well as economic and political discrimination.

At age four, Golda hid behind boarded-up windows and watched in horror as a mob of terrorist peasants surged through Kiev during bloody pogroms — looting, beating and stabbing any unlucky Jews on the street. It was a memory that stayed with her throughout her life.

"I can hear the sound of his hammer now, and I can see the children standing in the streets, wide-eyed, not making a sound, watching the nails being driven in," she said much later.

Moshe Mabovich sailed to America and, in 1906, he sent for his family. They settled in a small apartment at the rear of a store at Sixth and Walnut streets in a Jewish neighborhood of Milwaukee. Her father worked as a railway carpenter; her mother ran a neighborhood grocery store. Golda often arrived late for school because she had to help her mother in the mornings in the grocery.

But she excelled in school, learning English quickly. At age 10, she organized her schoolmates to provide textbooks for needy children.

She began studies at North Division High School in 1912 and wanted to become a teacher. But her mother, hoping that she would get married, made her quit school and go to work. When her mother tried to arrange a marriage with a real estate salesman fifteen years older, Golda fled in November 1912, to her older sister's home in Denver, Colorado.

She attended high school there and worked in her brother-in-law's dry cleaning business until her father wrote and begged her to come home. Returning to Milwaukee, she finished high school and attended Milwaukee Teachers' Training College.

But a different calling than teaching now beckoned Golda. She developed an interest in politics, joining the Paole-Zion, a group of labor Zionists who hoped to build a cooperative commonwealth in Palestine. Golda began speaking on street corners and, in 1917, she took a full-time, $15-a-week job with Paole-

Zion.

Her father didn't like her political activism at first. When he heard she was speaking on street corners, he hurried to find her, threatening to "pull her down from the platform by her braid." But when he arrived, he was impressed by her oratory and ended up applauding her speech instead.

Before she agreed to marry Morris Meyerson, a commercial artist, Golda demanded that he agree they would move to Palestine. The couple married on December 24, 1917, and, four years later, emigrated to Palestine, where they lived in a kibbutz near Nazareth. They worked every day draining swampland, in a region where malaria was so rampant that doses of quinine were provided with every meal.

"I was too tired to eat, but I ate anyway, so that others wouldn't say, 'The American girl can't take it,'" Golda later said.

After three years of Spartan and demanding kibbutz life, it was Morris who couldn't take it and the Meyersons moved to Tel Aviv to raise a family. Morris took a job as a bookkeeper. A son and a daughter were born and the family moved to Jerusalem. The family was extremely poor and Golda washed other children's clothes to pay for her children to go to nursery school. Her son, Menachem, became a cellist and headed Israel's Conservatory of Music. Her daughter, Sarah, became a kibbutz wife.

Fortunately for Israel and the world, Golda wasn't satisfied with the role of homemaker so she returned to politics. She was appointed to the Women's Labor

Council and later worked in the United States as a representative of the Pioneer Women's Organization.

Her renewed political activity put a strain on the marriage and her family. She separated from Meyerson in 1933 but they never divorced. He died in 1951 and Golda always kept his photograph in her bedroom.

Golda Meir

Her children also resented their mother's absences due to her political activism.

"My conscience about my children is only now at rest for the first time," she said at age 72. "They say they found the life I led so interesting but they didn't like being left so much. I tried hard not to be out except for work, not for social functions."

Golda became a leader in the Palestinian labor movement. She worked daytime for the Allies in World War II and, at night, helped smuggle Jews fleeing the Holocaust in Europe into Palestine. During a post-war trip to America, she raised $50 million in donations for the emerging nation of Israel.

A strong supporter of David Ben-Gurion's political faction, she was one of the signers of Israel's independence proclamation. But war broke out immediately after Israel gained its independence on May 14, 1948. In a last-ditch effort at preserving the peace, Golda disguised herself as a Bedouin woman and slipped across the border to meet with Jordan's King Abdullah, who told her it was too late for peace. During the conflict, Golda often smuggled guns beneath her skirts to Israeli soldiers.

Ben-Gurion, Israel's first premier, sent Golda to Moscow as ambassador to Russia. She spoke in Hebrew when she introduced herself at the Kremlin, even though Hebrew had been banned in Russia since the Soviet revolution. She went to a synagogue and found three hundred worshippers. The following week, forty thousand Jews showed up on Yom Kippur to catch a glimpse of the feisty new ambassador.

She returned home in 1949 and assumed the post of minister of labor. In 1956, she became the second woman in history to serve as a nation's foreign minister. Ben-Gurion once called her "the only man in my cabinet." At his urging, she changed her last name from Meyerson to the Hebrew name of Meir.

In 1957, she had the distasteful duty of announcing to the world that Israel would withdraw from the Sinai peninsula, which had been taken in war the previous year. She retired in 1966 to become secretary general of the Labor Socialist Party. She lost popularity for opposing the appointment of war hero Moshe Dayan as minister of defense and blamed him for splitting the party.

At age 70 in 1969, Golda Meir was called out of retirement, selected by the Israeli parliament to serve as the fourth prime minister, and she soon became a world leader. Despite the selection, her public approval rating was one percent. At the time, she was one of three women heads of state in the world.

She was then a short, plump, doddering grandmother with a lined face who wore shapeless dresses and kept her hair in a tightly wound bun.

But her foes often underestimated her. "She comes clumping along with that sad, suffering face drawn with pain from her varicose veins and God knows what-all," an opponent once said. "You rush to help her to her seat. She thanks you kindly. And the next thing you know, you're dead."

When Arab terrorists murdered eleven Israeli athletes at the 1972 Olympic games in Munich, Golda Meir declared that Israel would pursue terrorists "wherever they can be reached." Israeli forces raided Lebanon and Palestinian agents were killed in Europe as Golda ignored protests of the United Nations.

A meeting with Pope Paul VI did not go well. She viewed the pope as a symbol of Jewish persecution and wouldn't bear his criticism of her nation's military policies. To symbolize her disrespect, she refused to buy a new hat for the papal visit and, instead, had an old hat flown in from her homeland.

During the early 1970s, Golda Meir was ranked as the woman most admired by Americans in Gallup surveys. In 1975, she was named Woman of the Century by the Israeli Bonds organization. Even these honors she could not accept without comment.

"But do we really know all the women of the century and all that they have done?" she asked.

By the end of her tenure as prime minister in 1974, there were signs Golda was losing touch with the younger generation of Israeli's born in the homeland. Many were impatient with her tales of the pogroms and the old days.

For fifteen years, Golda Meir, a chain smoker who averaged three packs of cigarettes a day, suffered lympathic illnesses. She died in December 1978 of cancer at age 80.

With humble beginnings in Kiev and Milwaukee, Golda Meir evolved into truly a world citizen and, perhaps, even the woman of the century.

Bibliography

Articles published by *Appleton Post-Crescent*, Madison *Capital Times, Milwaukee Journal, Milwaukee Sentinel, Racine Journal-Times, Superior Evening Telegram, Time Magazine, Wisconsin State Journal.*

Blair, Hornberger, Stewart and Miller. *Literature of the United States.* Scott Foresman and Company, Glenview, Ill., 1966.

Bong, Carl and Mike O'Connor. *Ace of Aces: The Dick Bong Story.* Champlin Museum Press, Mesa, Ariz, 1985.

Bordin, Ruth, *Frances Willard: A Biography.* University of North Carolina Press, Chapel Hill, 1986.

Dictionary of Wisconsin Biography, The State Historical Society of Wisconsin, Madison:1960.

Famous Wisconsin Women, Vols. 4 and 5, Women's Auxiliary, State Historical Society of Wisconsin, Madison, Wis., 1975.

Goulden, Joseph C., *Korea: The Untold Story of the War,* Times Books, New York, 1982.

Holmes, Fred, *Badger Saints and Sinners,* E.M. Hale & Co., Milwaukee, 1939.

Lowry, Timothy S., *And Brave Men, Too,* Berkeley Books, New York, 1985

Wisconsin Women: A Gifted Heritage, Wisconsin State Division, American Association of University Women, Madison, 1982

Zeitlin, Richard, *Old Abe the War Eagle,* State Historical Society of Wisconsin, Madison, 1986

Index

More great reading by Marv Balousek

Here are three more compelling books by WISCONSIN HEROES author Marv

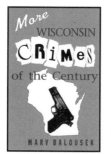

Balousek. *More Wisconsin Crimes of the Century* profiles 20 of the state's worst crimes and criminals, including Lawrencia Bembenek and Jeffrey Dahmer. *Honey, This is Trudy* is a mystery novel set in Madison in 1948 with the leading character based on a real crime reporter. *House of Alex* is a biography of Alex Jordan, the House on the Rock developer who was both a genius and a scoundrel.